A Harvest of Festivals

Longman Travellers Series

A Harvest of Festivals

MARIAN GREEN

Line drawings by Chris Williamson

Longman London and New York

Longman Group Limited London

Associated companies, branches and representatives throughout the world

First published 1980

British Library Cataloguing in Publication Data

Green, Marian
A harvest of festivals. – (Longman travellers series).
1. Folk-lore, English
I. Title II. Williamson, Chris
394.2'6942 GR141 79-40815

ISBN 0-582-50284-5

Set in 10/12pt V-I-P Palatino
Printed in Great Britain by
William Clowes & Sons Limited, London and Beccles

Dedication

To Brian Peacock and Beryl Mercer without whose help and inspiration this book could never have been written.

> And not by Eastern windows only,
> When daylight comes, comes in the Light.
> In front the sun climbs slow, how slowly,
> But Westward, look, the land is bright!
>
> *Say Not the Struggle Naught Availeth* A. Clough

Contents

Acknowledgements

The map on pages 54 and 55 is reproduced from the Ordnance Survey Map with the permission of the Controller of Her Majesty's Stationery Office, Crown Copyright Reserved.

Introduction

> Learn now the secret of the web that is woven between the light and the darkness; whose warp is life evolving in time and space, and whose weft is spun of the lives of men.
>
> Behold we arise with the dawn of time from the grey and misty sea, and with the dusk we sink into the western ocean, and the lives of a man are strung like pearls on the thread of his spirit; and never in his journey goes he alone, for that which is solitary is barren.
>
> *The Sea Priestess* Dion Fortune

This is a harvest of festivals, an experiential guide to some of the most fascinating celebrations of the battle between summer and winter, life and death, light and darkness. Britain, and England in particular (for this is the land I know best) is scattered with ancient ceremonies, modern revivals and reawakened versions of traditional feasts. Some are huge affairs, lasting several days and involving thousands of participants, others are brief, local festivals enjoyed by a mere handful of celebrants and their friends. There are many interesting, magical old festivals which are not mentioned here for I have tried to give the feeling of the activity, and some celebrations I have just not been able to attend.

If you can get the feeling of what it is like to join in these festivals, to encourage enthusiasm for these facets of our own heritage, then I have succeeded in my task. From humanity's most ancient concept of the meaning of life and the pattern of the seasons to the most recent ideas about time and space people have been striving to understand the mystery of day and night, sun and moon, earth and sky. Sometimes they have enacted the legends of the ancestral heroes, naming them as kings or saints, sometimes the village folk have got together to gather green branches as a sign of spring, to deck their houses and the streets,

sometimes they have linked hands and danced to celebrate the return of the strength of the sun.

Throughout these very varied festivals there are certain threads woven into a pattern. This was not clear when I began to write about these assorted feasts and the feel of the atmosphere when they are being celebrated. Gradually themes emerged, horses and dragons, serpents of dancers and processions of participants, circles of stones and spirals of celebrants, all symbolic of some overall key to what it is about. These different celebrations are about life and the overcoming of death. They take many forms, display different legends and myths, but the underlying design is there all the time.

By becoming civilised we have cut ourselves off from our traditional roots and our spiritual heritage and we are beginning to feel the loss. By taking a part, albeit only as an onlooker, at some of these festivals, both ancient and modern, we are taking a

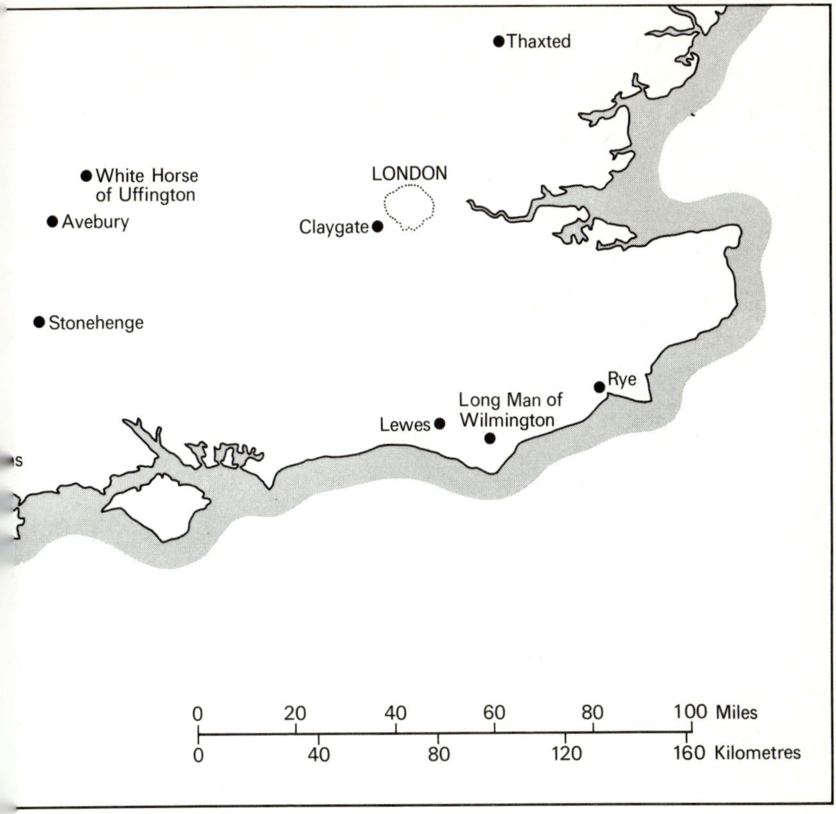

step to regain our inheritance, to rediscover that sense of wonder which can turn some ordinary event into a magical, memorable moment to be stored away and recalled in the dark days of winter. It is like that sudden burst of sunshine through a clouded April sky, or a first morning bird song in a city, a moment of sudden joy and delight. In the celebration of these festivals there may be many such moments of enchantment when your whole being is enthralled, your heart dances to the beat of the music and the mood of the feast. No one can gather in these moments for you. Neither television nor film can bring them to you, you must be there yourself, and from the wide field of experience gather in your own harvest of festivals. May the spirit of life bless your participation and bring you joy.

MARIAN GREEN
April 1979

CHAPTER 1

A Black Horse from the 'Golden Lion'

> I warn you young men everyone, For summer is acome unto day,
> To go to the green-wood and fetch your May home, In the merry morning of May
>
> *Padstow 'Morning Song'*

If you should find yourself, late one evening in spring, in the small, North Cornish seaside village of Padstow, you might witness one aspect of this country's heritage of ancient customs. On the night of 30 April, to be precise, you will find this normally quiet fishing village seething with life. The narrow, sloping streets are packed with local folk, and the 'Golden Lion' pub is jammed to the doors with swaying, singing folk, some still clutching pots of ale and hot pasties, although it is past eleven at night and the pubs should have closed ages ago.

There is an electrical excitement in the air, and people go by with armfuls of green branches and early spring flowers to deck the lamp-posts and doorways of the village, for this is the evening of the May Day appearance of the Padstow 'Obby 'Oss.

If you thrust your way into the crammed pub you will hear, above the clink of glasses and the rumble of Cornish voices, the strains of an accordion and the muffled thud of a big drum. Although the villagers may be singing ordinary West Country folk songs for a while, as soon as there is a lull the musicians return to the incessant, hypnotic beat of the 'Oss song which will reverberate through this part of the town for nearly 24 hours. At present they are just practising, warming up, getting ready for the great occasion.

In the narrow, crooked streets which meander down from the main road above the village the air of excitement is building up. Tonight there are many 'foreigners' about, as the Cornish call anyone from anywhere else, for this old traditional festival has brought pilgrims to witness the proceedings from all over the country. Towards midnight folk gather outside the 'Golden Lion', jamming the narrow roadway, thronging the pavements, leaning on the shop windows, everyone waiting for this festival garlanded with the blue and red handkerchiefs which are the tokens of the two sides in this strange survival.

Music strengthens and several accordions take up the tune. The players, suitably tanked up, come forth from the inn, their instruments forging a path to the street. It is May Day eve, and though the clean, white clothes of the real daytime part of the festival have not yet been donned, the folk are ready to begin. Houses and shops in this maze-like village are decked with bluebells, green branches and primroses. Bright yellow gorse flowers and young green leaves of sycamore trees have been bound to every convenient upright. The air is full of the smell of the sea, for the tide is in in the harbour (a fortunate thing for anyone unlucky enough to fall or be thrown in – some years a 10-foot fall into soft mud and broken bottles would be the lot of any reveller to go over the edge). The scent of the flowers carries on the cool wind, but suddenly no one is noticing the breeze or the flowers, for the throb of the drum has begun and the dancers of the day are starting their 'Night Song' to the heart-stirring drum beat and slightly uncanny tune. Pausing under the windows of the prominent folk of the community, the singers call to them:

> Rise up Mr . . . and joy you betide, for summer is acome unto day,
> And bright is your bride as she lies by your side,
> In the merry morning of May . . .

Around the town they go, waking anyone who has tried to go to sleep, pulling the legs of the local characters, ragging them in gentle or not so gentle jibes, urging them to witness the festival . . . 'the merry morning of May . . .'.

When the singers have completed their round they end up in the steeply sloping main square, between the fish and chip shop and the garage where five winding lanes converge. Here the great maypole has been set up, garlanded with hoops, higher than the cottages. Streamers from its flower-decked top stretch across the square, and during the night villagers will come bearing the tiny, curled yellow blossoms of the now rare cowslips to bind its lower part. How the local wine-makers must lament the use of these specks of spring-like blossom, yet the tradition is observed.

Night passes, black and blustery in the wind from the sea. The flowers and leaves wilt in the cool air, the strangers seek shelter in tents and coaches and cars in a vast car park above the village. At midnight it is half empty, at noon the next day there won't be room for another bicycle.

Soon after daybreak the village begins to stir; mostly it is the visitors who are up first, thronging the streets, wondering if the shops and cafés will open. The sun shines, as it usually does for these days of its worship, from time immemorial. Here and there among the crowd the white-clad participants, some sporting red, others blue favours, start to appear. The streets fill up, traffic is diverted, banks of watchers gather along every pavement, on every vantage point and windowsill. The business in the shops ceases for the doorways are crammed, and the shop assistants desert their posts to take part in the festival.

The 'Obby 'Oss and the Teaser whirl and bow before the gesturing dancers.

'BOOM, BOOM BA BOOM BOOM – BOOM BA BOOM BOOM' – the great drum thuds out its message, and all who hear begin to respond. The white-clad dancers swirl and bow, and from his hiding place behind the 'Golden Lion' the great black circular 'Obby 'Oss comes forth, led by the Teaser and the band of drums and accordions. It is not a hobby horse in the tradition of Morris dancing, a head on a pole with a cloak for the dancer, but a huge circular tarpaulin 'skirt' with a pointed black, red and white mask, capped with a plume of horsehair and ribbons. In front there is a small, sharp-beaked black head, its mouth gnashing hob-nail teeth, and at the back there is a beribboned tail. This mighty, fiendish disc sways and whirls from the shoulders of one of the team of dancers who will support it throughout the long day. "BOOM, BOOM BA BOOM BOOM" along the main street, down towards the harbour, up the steep slope of the square.

Now the words of the song have changed to the day song:

Unite and unite and let us all unite, for summer is acome unto day,
And whither we are going we will all unite,
In the merry morning of May. . . .

Again the villagers are encouraged to rise up and join the dance and the insistent beat, the echoing song in the narrow streets, the chanting crowds, the bowing 'Oss – all unite and unite. If you are there you have no option but to unite, for the throbbing rhythm, the surging people, the very air vibrating to the beat, draw you inexorably into the group soul of all participants.

Just as the song begins to seep out of your awareness through sheer repetition, it is subtly changed, the drum is stilled and the great black 'Oss sinks down. The tune, sung in a weird, lamenting minor key, changes:

O where is Saint George, O where is he, O?
He's out in his longboat all on the salt sea, O.
Up flies the kite, down falls the lark, O.
Aunt Ursula Birdhood, she had an old ewe,
And she died in her own park, O.

The Teaser kneels before the great disc of the Padstow 'Obby 'Oss. (*British Tourist Authority*)

A group of dancers sporting the coloured sashes of the Old 'Oss sway to the rhythm of the Day Song. (*Homer Sykes*)

Suddenly the heartbeat drum, the very centre of the united throng, begins again . . . 'Unite and unite and let us all unite . . .'. The 'Oss rises up and the dance goes onward. The darkness of winter has been overcome, the Saint is out fishing, all is well.

The old 'Oss is now no longer alone. His followers wear red, the colour of life. There is now a Blue 'Oss, a replica of the first, and his gang sports blue favours. He is known as the Temperance 'Oss, but both have their home pubs now. There is also a third 'Oss, for the children, about half the size and weight, and at times all three may be found swirling and swaying through the streets and up the hill, their music sometimes in harmony, sometimes against the beat, and the echoes fill the valley and the hearts of the people. You cannot avoid being involved, you cannot switch off the throbbing sound, for it reverberates your heartbeat, the pulse of the new life under the sun. The 'Oss of darkness has been overcome and the spring shall surely come again, even in the twentieth century.

All day the relays of dancers, young and old, fresh and weary, continue through the village streets, and across the valley, as they have done for many years. The crowds ebb and flow like the sea in the harbour, munching hot pasties, supping beer in pubs crammed solid with local folk and visitors, or herding in and out of cafés all day for that desperately-needed cuppa. Still the insistent beat is heard, now near, now distant, now blended and staccato as two groups dance in different areas of this echoing fishing port. Red and white and blue clothes of the dancers mingle with the rainbow hues of non-dancers; tiny children in their special get-up clutch at the gay belts and white-clad knees of their elders, each with his or her few drooping flowers. Even very small children of the village and surrounding area are involved. Some day they will grow up, and unless circumstances change, they too will surround the dark, sinister 'Obby 'Oss, and with gesture and mime beg the strange spirit of summer that it represents to return to the land, to bring fish to the local waters, to bestow on the folk all the good things it stands for. Light must overcome the dark or life will not continue; youngsters will have to carry on the tradition or it, too, may die. There seems little risk of this at present, for the 'harvest' reaped by the local shopkeepers and publicans on this occasion must be important to so small a place, where the fishing fleet is probably reduced to only a few boats, and 'Trips Round the Bay' is not a booming business.

The heartbeat throb of the drum becomes absorbed by those who stay all day, standing the pace of the dancing, or merely enduring the standing-about, watching and listening. It is like some great machine that pounds on, almost unnoticed until it stops, like the familiar ticking of a grandfather clock. Every so often there is a pause as the 'Oss sinks down, laid low by the Teaser's club, or drops with fatigue under the sheer weight of the tarpaulin disc which is whirled and flounced during the dance; then the throbbing drum is stilled, the accordions pause, and voices, growing harsher as the day progresses, sing the weird tune . . . up flies the kite, down falls the lark . . .'. Aunt Ursula Birdhood has a great deal to answer for. Seeming silence, punctuated by screaming gulls over the harbour, and the distant tinkle of music of a different tune from the roundabouts near the sea, then – 'THUD – BOOM BA BA BOOM' – it continues.

From early morning until late at night the untiring Padstow folk have their celebration, draining it and themselves to the lees, singing themselves hoarse for this strange horse-beast which is their symbol and centre-piece. There must be rivalry between the reds and the blues, both in the dancing and in the amount of cash they manage to collect into their clanking money-boxes, proffered to the crowd for donations. Usually there are a few scuffles when the pubs shut and the event has drawn to a close for another year. There has been tension all day, for any seriously observed ritual, understood or forgotten, is bound to heighten the feelings of the participants, and in the earliest days there would probably have been some sort of blood offering – the old gods were pacified and appeased with such sacrifices in times past.

As darkness falls and the lights in the village pick out the fluttering flags which cross the streets, spelling out naval messages few landsmen can read, scaring away demons, and brightening up this small town, the throb dwindles and gradually ceases. Gas lamps flare on the market stalls selling trinkets and hot dogs and candyfloss, and the rising tide in the harbour mirrors their assorted wares. The children's roundabout turns with its bright horses, but the dark, ancient 'Obby 'Oss has gone wearily back to his stable behind the 'Golden Lion' (which is surely the shining sun under a different guise). Tired dancers and visitors tramp on aching feet to find rest and relaxation in homes or cars – the carnival is over – at least until next year.

What is it all about, then? Is this a revival of some ancient pagan custom put on by the locals to encourage visitors, or a new way of attracting strangers and their money into a village which once thrived on the fishing industry? No – the ceremony is incredibly ancient, it is performed on 1 May each year by the villagers for the village.

There are many theories about the Padstow 'Obby 'Oss, and obviously the original reason for this festival to welcome summer has been overlaid with other, newer legends to try to make sense of the ancient custom. The words of the songs are now almost meaningless, and though historians and folklorists have debated their import, giving reasons and rightness to the modern, garbled survivals, the song has been sung, the dance danced and the folk united for time beyond remembering. What used to be sung may be lost for ever, but the implications are still there, summer is made welcome, winter driven back, and the strange, sinister 'Oss brings fertility and life to the land and sea.

May Day has always been a festival, celebrated all over the world, in some places as a folk festival, in others as a political rally. It is the first day of the summer, the Celtic Beltane, when

Some of the musicans and singers get carried away by the Padstow May Day Song. (*Homer Sykes*)

the Bel or Baal fires were lit as symbols of the bright Sun God, returned to life and strength at this time of year. When the first white, scented blossoms of the hawthorn broke forth there must have been rejoicing and merrymaking. May blossom is often thought unlucky when brought into the house, but that is because it is taboo. On the day of the May festival it would be a welcome sign of the turning year and the new, strong sun among the people. A taboo is broken once a year – the thing not done *is* done, ceremoniously and with recollection. May Day in Britain is too early for these sacred white flowers, but the feast is celebrated here.

The Padstow 'Obby 'Oss is by far the most important, most sinister and most real surviving tradition of May Day. It is a festival of the village folk and outsiders can at best only be the audience, though they will nonetheless be stirred by the occasion, thrilled by the vibrations of life and the returning sun.

Although the 'Oss rite for May Day is very, very old, it is hard to trace specific references to it except in the simplest form. In 1803 it was recorded in Rev. Richard Polwhele's *History of Cornwall* that a man dressed in the skin of a stallion was led through the streets of Padstow and dipped its head in every puddle and cast water over all those near it. In 1817 the man in the horse skin was the bringer of mirth and still given to casting dirty water in the faces of the laughing onlookers. Here a mention of 'songs made for the occasion' is given, and even then the report ends: 'The origin of this festival appears to be unknown.'

By 1824 the hoop-shaped horse covered with tarred canvas had arrived, and he was led through the town with a gathering of folk to a pool where he was supposed to drink and again cast water and mud over the spectators. At this time too, the story about the 'Oss and his party frightening away a French landing party who mistook his red-cloaked followers for soldiers, saw the light of day. The song seems to have acquired some of the words which are still used today:

> O where is Saint George, O where is he, O?
> He is in his longboat upon the salt sea, O.
> And for to fetch the summer home, the summer and the
>   May, O,
> For summer is acome, O, and winter is agone, O.

This was sung as the 'Oss was taken to Treator to drink at the pool.

In the mid-nineteenth century a sort of fair accompanied the 'Oss festival with ram-riding, effigies of unfaithful spouses set up in carts, and boys on donkeys making rough music, after the old 'Oss had returned to his stable. Later on in the last century there were cream teas and genteel dancing after the event with all the local folk dressed in their best. If the 'Oss was throwing muddy water about then he wouldn't have been so welcome, no matter what luck and fertility he was offering by his ritual act.

In about 1847 a local preacher, Thomas Tregaskis, offered the Mayers a roast ox if they would give up the pagan 'Oss dancing, but the folk preferred the dance to the bribe and the old rites continued.

The gradual change in form of the 'Oss seems to have reached its final phase at about this time. From an actual horse skin, which one presumes was roughly horse-shaped, to the great hoop, these days well over 5 feet in diameter, the change is complete. Swung from the shoulders of a dancer by stout straps, this huge

The maypole, decked with late spring flowers rears its head above the circle of cottages in Padstow.

construction is topped by an ancient, almost voodoo-like mask of black, red and white, and its small dragon/horse head shows hob-nail teeth in snapping jaws. Perhaps the colours echo the old Celtic symbols: black for death, red for life, and white for the sun, and the patterns painted on it are a faint recollection of the spirals which are found at ancient grave sites like Newgrange in Ireland, and on the ancient wayside crosses with which Cornwall abounds. Certainly the 'Oss is the nearest thing to a tribal mask, more familiar in Africa than in Europe, that one could encounter on a spring day. In some accounts the 'Oss was thought to represent evil or darkness, and was symbolically fought by the Teaser who still carries a club, though today this is stuffed with sheep's wool.

The maypole which features in Padstow's festival is another survival of a tradition which is found all over the country. Here the pole is very tall, and as Padstow was noted for fitting out ships in the era of sail, no doubt in the past the pole was a spare mast borrowed for the day. At one time sailors used to climb the pole to fix ribbons or flowers at the top, sometimes as much as 90 feet above the ground. It does not have woven ribbons like the inland maypoles, although streamers with flags, bunting and hoops filled with flowers (and these days, balloons, etc.) swing from the supporting wires high above the small square in Broad Street. Although maypoles were banned by Act of Parliament in 1644, they soon sprang up again once the people began to celebrate the old festivals, so no one knows how long this has been a feature of the Padstow May Day celebrations.

At one time there was only one 'Oss, but by 1903 mention of 'Osses and colts appears in the records, so the great 'Oss was no longer alone. In 1919 the Peace 'Oss made his appearance, beribboned in red, white and blue; he and his team collected for charity. He even appeared at the Royal Albert Hall in 1927 when people were taking an interest in the then disappearing folk customs. After the Second World War this 'Oss became known as the Blue Ribbon 'Oss, and still has an important place in the celebrations today.

The musicians used to play pipes and tabors and triangles; now it is a big drum and accordions, but the old, strange tune seems to be much the same.

Because people are interested in these old customs there is little fear that the Padstow 'Obby 'Oss will disappear; these days he finds it hard to carry his luck and fertility round his town due to the throngs of visitors who come for the day. The dancers and musicians are nearly all local folk, but it is impossible not to be caught up within the atmosphere, to be urged on by the pounding, exciting throb of the drum, and the incessant, repetitive tune. Even climbing the steep lane to the car park above the village on 1 May, trying to leave behind the surge and beat of the dance, you will hear, above the screams of the gulls flying in from the harbour, and over the trill of the robins, singing their territorial rights in the woods:

> Unite and unite and let us all unite, for summer is acome unto day,
> And whither we are going we will all unite,
> In the merry morning of May . . .

CHAPTER 2

St Michael and a dancing serpent

Dance, then, where ever you may be, For I am the Lord of the Dance, said he,
I'll lead you all, where ever you may be, I'll lead you all in the Dance said he.

Modern Folk Song

The West Country has a lot to offer followers of folk customs and those who like to be involved in person in ancient festivals. Cornwall is particularly rich in public celebrations, and as well as the Padstow 'Obby 'Oss, the inland town of Helston has its famous Furry Dance on 8 May. This is another occasion when a dance involves many of the local inhabitants, echoing the idea of the dance of life, and now at the very beginning of summer, the dancers welcome the strength of the returning sun. Whereas at Padstow the flower of the festival is the shy cowslip, here at Helston it is the sweet-scented lily of the valley, and all the dancers wear a spray of these delicate, creamy white bells. Even the local police, called in to keep the crowds off the roadways so that the serpent of tripping couples can move freely, sport sprays of lilies in their buttonholes.

To experience the real spirit of the Helston Furry it is necessary to be up early, and at the junction of Coinagehall, Meneage and Wendron Streets, or outside the Guildhall, decked all about its front with branches, bright yellow gorse and bluebells. A great banner below the clock proclaims the festival, and above it St Michael, the town's own patron, is depicted. He, too, has a place in this festival. The crowds are there very early, thronging streets decorated with green branches, along the roads of shops garlanded with flowers and greenery, for the first dance begins at 7 a.m.

At the early hour of 6.30 a.m. the car parks are already filling, and crowds gather on street corners near the Guildhall, where the first dancers and the Helston Town Band are getting ready for the great off. During the day the members of the Band will pass up and down the hills of this town many times, following different routes, with varying sorts of dancers in their wake, but now they are giving their shining instruments a last polish, adjusting their dark blue uniforms and the lilysprays in their peaked caps. It is likely to be cool this early summer morn. But the young men and women who are about to dance offer no concessions to the weather, the girls in bright summer dresses, the lads in white shirts and plain trousers, with dark green ties and the pale sprays of lilies of the valley.

Already tension is building up as the early-morning watchers

One of the Helston Town Bandsmen, sporting a spray of lily of the valley, watches the clock for the 7 a.m. start to the Furry Dance.

peer up at the Guildhall clock. The bandsmen come forth in dribs and drabs from the warmer, echoing hall, and the colourful dresses of the girls cluster like flower-beds at Kew, in gay greens and blues, pinks and golds. Many of the young ladies are wearing delicate sandals which hardly seem appropriate to a long dance, up and down the streets of this place, and even in and out of the houses and shops, but that is later. Now the long line of about 100 couples of lads and lasses from the area is forming up, and the long black minute-hand on the clock dial is creeping towards the 12. The Band gets into position, its bass drummer watches the clock-face, his drumstick raised, and the crowd holds its breath; then suddenly, as the minute-hand touches 12 and the clock begins to strike the hour, the bass drum thuds twice and the Band takes up the tune recently re-popularised by a band from elsewhere. DA DA DE DA DA DA – the silver trumpets, trombones and cornets launch into the refrain they will repeat hundreds of times between now and sunset. The dancers, clasping hands in pairs, emerge from the decorated doorway of the Guildhall to trip lightly the simple slip-steps, then swinging in and outwards, twirling round, changing partners, prancing onwards in a swaying column, all around the town. Their first dance takes them up Meneage Street and back again, diverging on the return 'leg' to dance around the grounds of Meneage Hospital. From the centre of the town, by a route which varies from year to year, they progress via Church Street and Cross Street to the bottom of the town, where flows the little River Cober on its way to Loe Pool. Here the dancers swing left and make their joyous way uphill to the Monument at the bottom of steep, wide Coinagehall Street, and thus back to the Guildhall.

The crowd, having let out a great gasp as the drum thudded its opening signal and the mellow music of the instruments took up the tune, surges along in the wake of the serpent of skipping dancers, or flows to find early refreshment from shops already sending forth welcoming scents of coffee and hot rolls. Along Coinagehall Street the market stalls have been set up, selling fruit and vegetables, crockery, cloth, whole-food goodies, and here and there the gay gewgaws which any festival attracts. The dancers have vanished into the throng but the music echoes strangely between the buildings, fading and recurring, as the Band leads among the narrow streets and lanes of Helston.

This is a charming inland Cornish town, honoured with Royal Charters since the time of King John in 1201, and well respected for its long involvement in the administration of Cornwall's tin-mining industry. This fact is recorded in the name of Coinagehall Street, where tin from Cornish mines was assayed and stamped for over 600 years. Nowadays the town probably draws quite a bit of its income from the flocks of tourists who visit the many shops, wander up and down the narrow lanes, and stay in pleasant bed and breakfast-type guest houses in the whole surrounding area. Some stray down to Gweek and look at the seals in their sanctuary there; others roam – usually in cars these days – the slender, twisting lanes of South Cornwall, which meander from hill to valley, exposing here and there, between high stone hedges, glimpses of views of sea or country, so delightful and, from such narrow vantage points, so swift in passing from view.

Helston itself is quite a gem of traditional small cottages interspersed with tall, narrow houses of the rural gentry of former years, many charmingly laid out with high rooms and elegant stairways, decorated ceilings and traditional woodwork. There are hidden gardens, protected from westerly winds behind high walls, which may be seen from higher streets which scramble upwards through this labyrinthine town. Alongside many of the roads of this place flows the kennel, the runnel of water named from the medieval sluice which maintained some degree of cleanliness in urban streets. Here the water is sparkling clear, but it can provide a surprise to unwary walkers with their eyes anywhere but on their feet, if the crowds are thick and the visitors are forced off the pavement edge. On Furry Day, Coinagehall Street is lined on one side with stalls and street vendors so this particular hazard is somewhat reduced, although in the narrow, steep lanes at the back of the town there is no such protection.

As you explore Coinagehall Street you may well notice a whitewashed pub called 'The Angel', which is tied in with Helston's link with St Michael. There are several legends which tell how the Archangel Michael and the Devil were fighting, and either Michael chased Satan away from Cornwall, or they were in the air above Helston and the Devil threw a rock at the Archangel – it may have been the lid of Hell. Anyway it missed, and now bits of it (perhaps it was a meteorite) can be seen built into the west wall of 'The Angel'. Have a look – they certainly don't look the same as the rest of the stone of the wall.

St Michael crops up later in the celebrations of Furry Day, but

ANGEL HOTEL
CAR PARK
ETS
HELSTON

there are still several dances to watch or follow. The second dance of the day is that of the children, held soon after 10 a.m. when, in recent years, nearly a thousand schoolchildren – the little girls dressed in white with circlets of flowers, different for each school, and the small boys in white shirts and shorts, again with their sprays of lily of the valley – dance hand in hand through the town. Sometimes the garlands are of real flowers, sometimes artificial, so it is possible now at the start of the growing year to see posies of roses, violets, bluebells and summer cornflowers decking the hair of these young ladies of the locality as they hop and skip the steps of the Furry Dance. Somehow they manage to smile, though the dance, albeit somewhat shorter than those performed by the adults, is long for their small legs, and the sun usually shines on their sparkling white outfits. Each year a different school has the honour of leading the trailing serpent of children, and the first dancers in the line are chosen for the greatest honour of all. (In all the dances it is traditional that the first two couples must be Helston-born.) It can be no easy thing to have to dance along rough streets before a live audience of thousands, and not trip or spoil the pattern by losing step. Amid oohs and aahs from admiring parents, relatives and friends, these small dancers skip their way down to the gardens of Lismore for a brief rest and refreshment. In this age of jeans and denim it is a change to see a large number of smartly dressed youngsters participating in this, their own town's festival, and they do seem to enjoy it.

Once the children have danced away, accompanied by an augmented Band and flanked at intervals by teachers carrying tape-recorders so that all may be able to hear the music, it is certainly time for many of the spectators to seek their own refreshment, whether it be late breakfast, early lunch, or simply a mid-morning snack. One of the best places to go is the big church hall in Coinagehall Street, where efficient Methodist ladies and gentlemen lay on a vast array of sandwiches, cakes and of course in this part of the world, Cornish pasties. Eaten hot enough to burn your fingers, they are an ideal counter to the chilly winds which may be blustering among the throngs absorbed in the activities of the dancers.

The most famous dance of the day is the Midday Dance when

The Children's Furry Dance goes up Coinagehall Street, in front of the 'Angel Inn' and market stalls. (*Brian Shuel*)

The leaders of the Midday Helston Furry Dance begin the Spiral in the gardens of Lismore. (*Homer Sykes*)

the gentlefolk of the area come forth in morning dress, the gentlemen in grey toppers and tails, and the ladies in long, elegant summer frocks with picture hats and matching gloves. In this day and age it is a very rare sight, especially in a fairly remote corner of the West Country. It looks like the greatest society wedding of all time, without a bride and groom. I imagine every dress-hire company in Cornwall provides the costumes for these dancers, although regular participants may well have their own outfits – well, the men, anyway – none of the ladies would wear the same dress year after year.

This is the most solemn and sedate of the versions of the dance. The music and rhythm are the same, but now the dancers are the captains of local industry, business and professional people, even senior naval officers from nearby Culdrose; more mature persons for the most part, who look right in the sombre attire of the formal morning dress. Their steps are stately and correct but they are all smiling, and the ladies in the swaying, whirling column listen intently for comments about their dresses and hats as they progress along the streets. This surely must be part of the fun of the occasion. Maybe this year's hat is a little too much, or the neckline of the gown a trifle on the daring side – what does it matter? – it is part of the festival tradition.

Why then get up in this somewhat outmoded gear and prance through the streets on 8 May? Again, all concerned are celebrating the return of life after the death of winter, the beginning of the growing season, the start of summer's warmth. This dance is eternal, and because it is a religious rite, far older than Christianity, it is traditional to put on one's best clothes and become a worshipper at the altar of the Creator. Branches of new-grown leaves are in abundance, the attractive colours and designs of the ladies' dresses reflect the spirit of nature which will gradually, almost imperceptibly, clothe the barren winter trees with green, shroud the verdant fields with yellows and pinks and blues of spring flowers. As they come forth decked out in their spring finery so the dancers echo the idea of the eternal, changing dance of life; dark and bright, sombre and gaily coloured, the ladies and gentlemen whirl in expressions of this selfsame principle. The constant change from day to night and back to day; spring ripens into summer, mellows into autumn, withers into winter, then blossoms into spring again. Perhaps this is what the dark, formal attire of the gentlemen, and the bright glowing colours of the ladies' gowns are meant to represent.

The dancers follow-my-leader behind the Band, up and down the streets, in and out of the houses and gardens, bringing the celebration of life and summer warmth both indoors and out in the open. Driving away the dregs of winter and the spirit of the

Dark One who brings the long nights and cold winds, celebrating the return of the life-force throughout the town. This particular dance has a special feature too, which to me is a confirmation that the celebration is concerned with the living power of nature. The skipping and spinning column of dancers finally enters Lismore's fine gardens, and in the centre, within the cup of a natural amphitheatre of smooth lawns, they dance into a spiral, and continue, drawing the coils tighter and tighter, with the Band standing to one side, until they are all treading the turf of the lower lawn. Then, with a final boom from the drum, they stop – dead. There is a moment's pause, then the laughing, excited dancers break away from the serpent of pairs to seek rest and refreshment before reassembling to complete their dance. They do not unwind the spiral. The spring has been wound up, exactly as it is in Africa where village maidens, dressed in their festival finery, draw the spiral with their bodies; like the whirling dervishes who spin to encourage the creative spirit to stay with the world and bring inspiration and life to the faithful.

People of many countries dance this way in their oldest celebrations, and here we know the spiral is an ancient symbol of great importance, for it is carved clearly upon the mighty stones at Newgrange in Ireland. Upon the doorsill of one of the most ancient buildings in the West, raised over 5,000 years ago, the sacred spiral has been patiently chipped on a large boulder, above which there is a roof box of flat stones through which the midwinter sunrise shines into the passage of this megalithic structure. Again it is a combination of the light of the new year, there at its very birth, being linked with the spiral form, as if it is possible to draw in a supply of the life-force and lock it safely in stone or garden for the whole year. Certainly, if you are able to find a place on the grass above this dell to wait for the dancers to arrive, heralded by the music of the Band, you will be able to experience for yourself the strange feeling as if the whole area were breathing in, as the ladies and gentlemen curl ever more tightly into the centre. It is a really magical moment, in a day of delight.

The last dance of the day, performed by the early morning dancers, begins at 5 p.m. By now many of these participants must be weary, having danced a long route earlier on, and probably put in a day's work in shop or bank – though not in office or factory, as most of the local ones close for the day. The Band, too, must be beginning to feel it would like to put its many pairs of feet up, like some long-distance centipede, and lay down its heavy, shiny collection of instruments. Nevertheless the folk still have a spring in their step, a smile on their faces, and probably the feeling of something well done. There must be a kind of satisfaction involved in the participation in these rural festivities, a warm sensation around the heart that the thing has been done properly, with a wholeheartedness which is obvious to the audience. The flowers which deck the shops and businesses are beginning to droop, the stalls with their merchandise are packing up and allowing more space on the pavements, and the westering sun catches on rooftops and gleams through chinks between the buildings as it sinks towards the encircling hills. Still the DA DA DE DA DA DA of the Band can be heard, with the matching patter of many footsteps, and the chatter and giggles of the crowds. Until the last note is blown, the last whirl of paired dancers completed, the festival of Furry is not ended.

In the morning, as well as the early dance and the chain of children, in quieter backstreets and squares a different tune is heard. It is more haunting, faery-like and strange, piped by recorders and sung by young voices, accompanied by mime and the clash of tambourines. Within a ring of green branches, carried from time immemorial by heralds as a sign of peace, a space is cleared so that the players can act out another fragment of the story of spring. This is the enactment of the Hal-an-Tow play, usually performed by senior students and staff of local schools, supported by members of the Helston Old Cornwall Society. Upon a 'stage' cleared among a forest of waving branches of new-leafed sycamore, a troupe of brightly costumed players acts out the words of a simple song with a silly, nonsense chorus. Certainly the theme of the story is very old, for it is mainly concerned with fights between an assortment of protagonists, from Spaniards versus English or Cornishmen, to Archangel Michael and Satan. Dark and light, life and death, the eternal battle which most of these festivals are concerned with, in one way or another.

The first rendering of the play is at 8.30 a.m. on St John's Bridge at the bottom of the town, when the young folk return from the woods with green branches used gently to herd people away from the play area and form a sort of walking forest of protection around the players. To the accompaniment of recorders a chorus sings a rather high-pitched tune, and as each verse is heard the appropriate characters enact the story. There are five verses usually sung today; the first deals with Robin Hood and Little John, who have gone to the fair, but the chorus intends to follow them to the greenwood, hence the branches, and chase the buck and doe. Traditional heroes of Britain, Robin Hood and his Merrie Men appear in all sorts of guises in folk plays, and Maid Marian is another version of the Goddess of the Woodlands and Wildthings, so here is the first link with the ancient legends. The second verse is concerned with the Spaniards, who are accused of boasting and are condemned to eat 'the grey goose feather' (i.e. arrows) 'and we will eat the roast, O'. Here some dismal-looking Spanish prisoners are led on, but no roast goose seems to be forthcoming!

The third verse brings us back to the Mummers, for we have St George and a splendid dragon with whom he does battle and wins. St George for Merry England is dressed in shining silver mail with a white surcoat, the dragon is scarlet and scaly with huge, saucer-like eyes. While the chorus sings they tussle for domination, but eventually St George's sword makes a fatal thrust and the dragon is overborne. The victor 'is the right, O, in every land . . . where e'er we go'.

Next to take the stage is Helston's own saint, the mighty Michael, and his traditional adversary is Satan, here clad in black and purple, with horns and tail against the gold and scarlet of the Archangel's armour.

> But to a greater than Saint George, our Helston has a right, O,
> Saint Michael with his wings outspread, the Archangel so
> bright, O,
> Who fought the fiend, O, of all mankind the foe.

Again they do battle, and after a noisy struggle Michael's trusty spear lances through the Lord of Darkness and down he falls. Interesting that Michael is greater than St George, but not surprising, for Michael has taken over where many of the pagan sun gods left off. He crops up time and again in one guise or another at these ancient festivals.

The last verse somehow seems to reflect the nonsense rhymes of the Padstow song, for here we have 'Aunt Mary Moses', rather like 'Old Ursula Birdhood'; some sort of nature spirit impersonated as an old hag, or perhaps a remembrance of the Lady Mary who is herself a version of an older maid/mother goddess. Here Aunt Mary Moses 'and all her power and might,

St George tackles the Dragon in the ancient Hal-an-Tow play at Helston. (*Packet Newspapers, Falmouth*)

O', occurs, and a blessing of God is asked for her and for 'peace in Merry England, both day and night, O, both now and evermore, O'.

Much of the actual chorus between verses is the frequently found meaningless jumble of words:

> Hal-an-Tow, jolly rumble O, for we are up as soon as any day, O,
> And for to fetch the summer home, the summer and the May, O,
> For Summer is a-come, O, and Winter is a-gone, O.

Probably the original words of the whole song have undergone many changes since the festival was first celebrated, and no one knows when that was. Time before remembering is the usual sort of dating for these traditional rites, and except for wars and plagues most of them have been carried on each year since. Whatever the original words were, the feeling is there, the notion of heroes who fight dragons or devils of darkness and bring back light and life with the springtime – a rite as old as the hills and surely marked in some way since there were folk on them who sought to encourage the young sun, and give thanks for his returning strength.

At the Helston Festival we have both the threads which have been traced through the festivals in this book, the strand of dance, and the idea of the dragon or horse which is the darkness of winter and is overcome by the hero. Every one of these celebrations has slightly different customs woven into it, but each is part of the picture of the most ancient rite of all – the welcoming of the spring. Today we take it for granted, but in times past, folk relied for their very survival on the new growth of vegetation, the return of the wandering herds of wild creatures upon which they depended for food. Sometimes the festival took place in midwinter at about the time we celebrate Christmas, a few days after the winter solstice, that point in the sun's journey through the sky when it begins to rise higher in the heavens each day to its zenith at midsummer. Each day is a little longer, and hope returns. Other festivals were held when the flocks and herds carefully tended through the winter began to drop their young, or when the first flowers were seen shyly poking through the snow, indicating that the archetypal Earth Mother was coming back to the people to make the land green and the livestock fertile.

In the West particularly the feast seems to have been held early in May, perhaps when the foaming white blossoms of the hawthorn began to cover the hedges and throng in the coppices. This tree has often been associated with healing, and in some places it was customary to tie shreds of cloth or ribbons to a thorn tree and ask for healing. As the cloth was blown away the disease was thought to abate. Some say its intoxicating scent is like that of a plague-ridden town, yet its name, quickthorn, relates to life, as in 'the quick and the dead'. Children eat its early green leaves, calling them 'bread and cheese'; probably many of the old country folk were glad to find anything to eat during the 'hungry gap' between January and May.

In Helston the Furry Dance is always held on 8 May, unless this date falls on a Sunday or Monday (the latter being Helston's cattle-market day), for that was the Feast of the Apparition of St Michael who appeared at least four times on this date. In A.D. 391 he visited Monte Cargano near Brindisi; in A.D. 715 he appeared on Mont St Michel off the coast of Brittany; in A.D. 590 it was the turn of San Angelo in Rome, and he came to the Cornish St Michael's Mount, so legend has it, in A.D. 495. Michael has been the patron saint of Cornwall from very early times, probably before the Norman Conquest. It is appropriate that such a mighty archangel should be associated with overcoming darkness and winter in this western land.

If the festival was originally linked with the first blooming of the maytree then it has moved back, for the hawthorn flowers, even in the mild weather of Cornwall, are seldom seen in any quantity until mid or late May, but perhaps a single open flower was sufficient to get the celebrations going long ago. The Church adopted many of the older, pagan customs, for St Augustine encouraged the young Christian Church in the sixth century to use places and dates which were already sacred and familiar to the folk for the major feasts of the calendar. If there was already a spring gathering and feast then it was worth keeping up, but Christianising in form. Probably the local pagans didn't take much notice of this but kept the festival in their own way. Kipling has something to say about it:

> Oh, do not tell the Priest our plight, or he would call it a sin,
> But – we have been out in the woods all night, a-conjuring Summer in!
> And we bring you news by word of mouth, good news for cattle and corn:
> Now is the Sun come up from the South, with oak, and ash, and THORN!

Helston Town Band still acknowledges 1 May by playing its tune in the streets morning and evening as a rehearsal, but the dances, the folk-play and all the real festivities are held over until 8 May. No one knows for certain where the tune came from, although it seems to be old, and various versions of it occur in folk dances all over the country. Traditionally the modern bandsmen learn their parts from each other rather than a written score (for in such a way all ancient knowledge was passed down, keeping such mysteries from others who could read), the bandmaster being responsible for ensuring that the tempo and spirit of the music are preserved. Although there have been recordings made by other bands, these do not have the authentic feeling of the band which is prepared to march all day, up and down steep streets, in and out of houses and gardens, a total of over 16 miles, to bring luck and success to the whole town. The words of a song sung to a version of the Furry Dance are fairly modern, written in 1906 by a Miss Katie Moss, and they have no place in the real, traditional Furry Dance celebrations in Helston. The original is Helston's tune, to celebrate with joy the conquest of winter by spring, the cold death by the warm, new sun.

The name 'Furry' is possibly derived from the Latin word *feria* meaning a fair or holy day, usually of a religious nature. The dance has also been known as 'Faddy' which may have some connection with an ancient English dance called 'The Fading'. There was also an old Irish name, *Rinnce Fada,* the Long Dance, from which this 'Faddy' title may have come. Another popular name is Flora Day, or the Floral Dance, under which name the written words of the song are usually known. This would relate to Flora, the Roman Goddess of the spring and flowers, and was popularly used in Helston in the eighteenth, nineteenth and early twentieth centuries, probably deriving from eighteenth-century interest in all things of the classical period, including history and architecture. Wherever the name derives from, it has been heard all over the world, and is surely remembered by exiled Helston folk wherever they go. In some countries they have got together to celebrate the dance and traditions of their home town on 8 May, but the Furry, or Faddy, or Floral Dance has really got only one home of its own.

Helston does celebrate a fair in the traditional way, for as well as the four dances weaving through the narrow streets, and the merry Hal-an-Tow players in their colourful medieval costumes and green branches, at the bottom of the town there is a fair with its circling roundabouts bearing plunging horses. A fine old mechanical organ produces the special evocative music, a great attraction to some visitors who are drawn by the metallic tunes, the automated clashing of cymbals, the whistles and the mechanical drums which all add to the atmosphere of fun-fair.

The Guildhall at Helston is decked with flowers and flags for the May Furry Dance each year.

There are plenty of different sorts of entertainments – shooting galleries and penny-in-the-slot machines, as well as stalls selling all the fare of the fair, and souvenirs of the occasion.

If you happen to have a longing for an early holiday, or wish to visit some quieter corners of the West Country, between the Padstow 'Obby 'Oss Festival and the Helston Furry Dance you will have a good week to explore this fascinating area with its many delightful villages, its old customs, fresh fish, clotted cream, and Cornish pasties. Each of these celebrations is worth the trip, and if you can manage both that is a bonus. Each is a representation of the triumph of life over death, spring over winter; each has its own symbol and customs. Padstow is wild and blatant with its red and white dressed dancers led by its small, informal band and its weird, ancient 'Obby 'Oss with his

Teaser, an archaic, archetypal figure who might be Winter himself. Helston is sedate, the dancers dressed in spring finery or formal morning attire, tripping hand in hand, whirling in folk dance sets, in and out of houses and shops to bring, symbolically, the new life of the year, everywhere they go. There is joy in the streets of both places, and always it is the local folk who lead the dances, play in the bands, and deck the houses and lamp-posts with fresh greenery, but it is a very different feeling. Both have a magic that makes the heart rise at the sound of the music, both impel the feet to step in time to the drums, and both cause the spectators to smile and sense the atmosphere, all the way through.

People may not remember the ancient traditions, and indeed many visitors who find themselves involved in these festivals of dance and music are surprised by all the activity. On the other hand there are people who travel hundreds of miles, even from across the sea, to be in the right place on the right day. It is possible to see the festivities on television, or read about them in newspapers, but to be there in person to watch the dancers face to face, hear the throb of the drums, the impulsion of the music, is a very different thing. After all, no one could really quibble with the motive:

For we are up as soon as any day, O,
And for to fetch the Summer home, the Summer and the
  May, O,
For Summer is a-come, O, and Winter is a-gone, O.

CHAPTER 3

Ancient Avalon, new Jerusalem and modern Glastonbury

> Trackway and Camp and City Lost, Salt Marsh where now is corn –
> Old wars, old peace, old Arts that cease, And so was England born.
> She is not any common Earth, Water or Wood or Air,
> But Merlin's Isle of Gramarye, Where you and I will fare!
>
> *Puck's Song* R. Kipling

Under a blue summer sky, against a background of ancient stonework of the largest abbey in England, a troupe of actors and actresses plays out the stories of history and religious tradition. In soft Somerset voices they re-enact those old miracle plays which brought the Bible to the people, particularly in the Midlands and North. There, each guild of craftworkers taking a particular part of the Old or New Testament, acting on the back of a wagon or farm cart in market places, the grounds of big houses, or in the streets, retold the tales of God and Man and the Son of Man. Nowadays this occurs in a more rural place, perhaps even the place where some of the legends, perhaps not recorded in the Good Book, but in the hearts of the people, were acted out in reality. Did that wandering trader, Joseph from Arimathea come to these islands in his quest for tin, with the Phoenicians, who sailed their small boats to this now landlocked harbour? Did he perhaps, on one of his journeys bring his young relation Jesus, the son of Mary, a carpenter's wife from Nazareth, to visit this rainy, green land where water was more common than dry ground, and mists and damp hid the light of the sun? Did he plant his thorny staff in a hillside above the lapping waters of the mere, and find it rooting and flowering though so far from its warmer home?

There are many questions about Glastonbury. Some have been unravelled a little, only to disclose more enigmas, more puzzles, more legends entwined in real history. From this grassy, glassy isle of Avalon tales have been spread across the whole of Christendom, yet even at the time of Jesus the communities had been long established in a marshy, waterlogged area, very different from the green pastures you see here today. Certainly the strange pyramidal shape of the Tor still haunted the

A scene from one of the Miracle Plays acted within the vast ruins of Glastonbury Abbey. (*Brian Walker*)

landscape, within its distant circle of wooded hills; but at its feet, instead of level fields dotted with fine Friesian and Ayrshire cattle, there were swamps with alder scrub, birches and deep, peaty pools, the colour of strong, black coffee, which at night flickered with the will-o'-the-wisp of blue marsh-gas flames. Here in this uninspiring, reedy lakeland, villages had been built on small islands, banked with clay, ringed round with palisades of stout logs and defended with narrow causeways, straight as a die, constructed of brushwood and imperishable alder. These roadways still exist, buried under the modern tarmac, and rimmed with pollarded willows whose bent and man-tortured shapes loom over stagnant ditches and seem to lurk in the mists of this shadowy land.

Where to begin the story of this place whose atmosphere, to some, is filled with strangeness, whose legends are known to children all over the land (though they may not be aware of the setting), whose hills and wells have witnessed aspects of Britain's Christian history from earliest times? Perhaps we might return to the actors at their summer revels. For a number of years the ruins of the great abbey have been the ideal setting for the performance of the miracle plays. Some of these stories tell of the birth of Jesus, or the Shepherds' play, or Herod's tale, or the coming of Joseph of Arimathea with his holy symbols. At other times the secular tales are presented, tales of Arthur and Guinevere who are closely linked with this place, of Merlin, and of the Holy Grail and the questing knights. Or we might witness the stirring story of Arthur's last battle, concluding with his departure in the arms of the three dark queens, carried by a boat of glass to an island in a lake, where he rests among the sacred apple trees until he is needed again, to fight the last great battle of light against night.

Among the bones of that once-great abbey whose stones glow honey-coloured in the evening light, the troupe of actors comes, to pipe and drum, to bring the stories and music of a bygone time to the watchers. Most of the players are local folk, and their own accents add reality to the tales they tell. Did not Middle or Old English sound something like these soft country voices, and did not our ancestors speak in the manner of these gentle West Country folk? The lines of the plays may not be ancient, although certainly some of them date back to the Middle Ages. Perhaps the audiences now are much quieter, more attentive as they sit in the shadows of the standing masonry of the twelfth century, than would have been folk of earlier times. The stories are not new to us today, but they do serve as reminders of some of the things which actually happened in this area, as well as of those events which legend places here, in times past.

Some of the plays that have been enacted upon this sacred turf come from the Wakefield Cycle of Mystery Plays, and in word and song, dance and mime, tell to the people the entire history of the Bible, from the Creation of Adam to the End of the World. God speaks to the people here in a place where the people have spoken to God since His message was revealed to them nearly 2,000 years ago, through the coming of the first followers of Christ. Some of the plays, usually performed in pairs, are of more recent derivation than are those from the medieval manuscripts. Some tell of the saints who visited Glastonbury, including St Patrick, and St Dunstan who was one of its abbots. Others re-enact the Grail Mysteries and the Play of Arthur. All appeal not only to the senses of sight and hearing, but to those inner senses that detect the reality of myth, the validity of legend, where word or action can bring a lump to the throat, a tear to the eye. There is no feeling of desecration as the players dance and sing where once the choirs of monks chanted their litanies; rather it is a revival of the spirit of the place, and the light which must have streamed through glorious stained glass windows is not filtered, except by scudding clouds. Towards sunset the reddening west makes a splendid backdrop to the actors, and the stones of the old abbey shadow purple patterns on the greensward.

If you have time to stroll about the ruins before the play begins you will find the only whole building is the Abbot's kitchen. A huge square building of the fifteenth century, with a pointed roof and lantern, it seems like a vast space capsule, just ready to launch from the mown turf into the blue sky of a summer evening. Inside it is cool and very much like what an alchemist's laboratory may have been like, with deep ovens, a rill of water, and a high tapering ceiling supported on stone groins which seem almost to spiral upwards like a rifle barrel, into the dark lantern. The circle is squared here, for the room is four-sided, but it turns to eight and then to a circle with its pointed spire. The Abbot's kitchen? – I wonder! It would seem a shame to use this place for something as mundane as cooking.

Probably the festival of plays in the abbey ruins, which happens each July to August, is not so great an event, but there is something extremely compelling about sitting in the centre of the stage of such action where myth and history blend. It is intriguing to watch the players, descendants perhaps of the original folk who lived in these lowlands, performing what to us is either legend come to life, or some sort of pantomime based on hearsay and fairy tales. Does it matter? You come to Glastonbury in obedience to your heart, not your head. Maybe you wander westward and find that a meander away from the motorway brings you into these quiet lanes, or perhaps you are drawn by the legends themselves, or the religious gathering at midsummer.

This is a real festival, when the Anglican Pilgrimage takes place on the last Saturday in June. Thousands of clerics, supporters and lay Christians make the long journey by car and coach, on foot or bicycle (though not by rail, as there is no railway nearer than about 12 miles). Each congregation carries its banner, handsomely worked by church ladies. Some are modern, some ancient, some pictorial, some symbolic; Matthew, Mark, Luke, John, St Saviour, St Michael and all angels, the Archangel Gabriel; some are the flags of town churches, shaking the soot of London from their silken folds; some are country banners, accustomed to the winds of the western lands. Each has its honoured bearer and two supporters, a trinity to uphold each church. Priests come forth in all their finery, cassocked and coped, mitred and biretta'd, in surplices and albs of incredible magnificence. They carry thuribles and censers, candles in elaborate brass and glass lanterns which twinkle in the midsummer sunlight.

Scarlet and gold, silver and azure blue, the colours of stained glass reflected in rich fabrics skilfully worked into great banners, throng the streets, and the sweet, cloying scents of many different incenses blend and surge on the wind. Such a panoply of clergy is assembled that the streets of Glastonbury look more like a festival in Rome. Here and there bunches of the faithful strike up a hymn tune to keep the spirit of the occasion. In the car park, clerics of all ranks are eased and assisted into brocaded regalia, laden with bullion and sparkling with precious metals, each trying to outshine his fellows on this festive day. Lady attendants tweak stoles into alignment, polish brass ferrules on the banner poles, and proffer tablets of black charcoal to fire the swinging thuribles.

Above the heads of the gathering crowd around St John's Church in the High Street, near the Holy Thorn, the swaying banners mass and throng like the war flags of some gathering army, or like the wings of the choirs of angels which many of their symbols depict. Haloes glitter with gold and jewels, madonnas

The Holy Spirit descending upon Glastonbury embroidered on one of the many banners carried during the annual Anglican Pilgrimage in June.

smile serenely upon the watching folk, crucified figures suffer and seem to spill their gemmed blood droplets upon the waiting crowd. Martyrs display their wounds and torments, angels hover, saints aspire upward in silks and satins, velvets and brocades as the procession forms outside the church. Watchers balance precariously on the churchyard walls to get a glimpse of their own church banner, or clamber on convenient table tombs beside the path. A great mass of clergy lines up, each banner carried on high by its strong bearer, supported by twin acolytes who grasp silken cords to stay it against the wind, or catch the flapping fringes lest they disrupt the parson's head-gear. Hymns are sung in a kind of unison, and the words, like the incense fumes, rise upward towards a thundery sky. Sky blue is echoed on banner and cope, but heavy clouds threaten a summer storm, and distant thunder resounds against the organ of St John's.

Gradually the throng settles into a coherent, orderly form as its colourful components take up their positions. It is like the arrangement of some mysterious battle, the troops of Light massing against a darkening sky. Pale incense smoke wafts upwards, a strange blend of frankincense and myrrh, the golden censers swinging and chains clinking as the clergy move off on their short procession along Glastonbury's sloping High Street. Soon, like some winged and jewel-scaled serpent, the cavalcade unwinds to the tune of 'He who would valiant be', coming hither in a great pilgrimage of faith and duty.

The less exotically dressed followers, the choristers in their black and blue and purple cassocks and white surplices, ruffed and starched like courtiers in the reign of Elizabeth I, join the caravan of light. It passes through the great arched gates of the abbey, which in their day must have witnessed many similar events, both Catholic and Protestant. The oaken doors are held back as one by one, the saints and angels dip briefly to enter the archway, high above their heads; embroidered chalices and sacred hosts worked in silks and silver thread dim in the shadow of the gateway and then pass on again into the light of day to sparkle in the sunlight which still strives against the threatening thunder-clouds.

Within the stones of the abbey, spectators of hundreds of years of Christian ritual, the congregation, sorts itself out for an open-air service. In the grass-floored nave choirs form to sing to the Almighty, prayers echo through the PA system, thanksgiving and worship resound from the mighty throng, probably one of the largest gatherings of worshippers except for Christmas. Under the spreading chestnuts, village parsons stand; here and there Anglican nuns kneel on long-hallowed turf where saints and kings have lain buried until other kings have ordered them displaced.

Across the greensward lost children yell, dogs yap, hymns rise up to the Creator, and everyone is looking forward to a cup of tea and a sit-down after a long wait. The turf is smooth, the air is still within the encircling sacred walls, and the rain is still holding off. Incense smoulders out, unattended during the service. Gradually the atmosphere unwinds; the pomp and circumstance ease, and priests, their sacred duty duly performed, acknowledge their parishioners who have come all the way from home to this obscure Somerset town for a day of prayer and procession. As a spectacle it would be hard to beat, and as those heartfelt songs of praise rise up, there is a certain feeling in the air which is so often missing from the local church evensong. The whole place seems filled with an atmosphere of the splendour and ancient pageantry with which legend would credit it. If Arthur's Court was in this area, and Camelot had really looked like its Hollywood film sets, then it would surely have been as filled with banners and elaborate caparisoning such as are to be seen in the town this midsummer day.

The entire place is a kind of rampart of faith and hope against the encroachment of darkness and ignorance. Throughout its long recorded history Glastonbury has been a defence of the faith or of the people. The earliest settlements in the area, down in the marsh at Meare and Godney, are man-made islands built as a defence against invaders, yet providing a protected homestead in a lake which gave bountiful supplies of fish and waterfowl. No doubt these lowlands had Nature's own protection, too.

The modern Anglican pilgrims are the latest in a long line of the faithful who have made their way to this strange land of mist and enchantment, to worship and witness such of the mysteries as man can see and perceive. It is a strange place of unlikely vistas, weird light, and changeable weather, for the elements have not been tamed here. From the ring of surrounding hills, whichever way you come, there is the verdant lowland, criss-crossed with water ditches, called 'rhynes' hereabouts, each with its fringe of pollarded willows and alder scrub; but in the centre, like the set for a science fiction film, a strange green hill rears up. It is as if some primeval monster is arching up from the grassy pastures, crowned now with a square tower. Although the cock-eyed pyramidal Tor is the most obvious feature of this uncanny landscape, it has two acolytes. To one side is the rounded, smooth Chalice Hill, and on the other, reaching out towards the more prosaic village of Street, is Wearyall Hill. Each has its own story to tell, each has seen visitors from afar, treading tired from a long journey; each has been a sort of refuge to the small ships which sailed over these lands before the sea wall was built, and canals dried out the fields.

'There is a green hill far away, without a city wall . . .' This could so easily be Glastonbury's Tor. The town sprawls at its feet and stretches up the flanks of Wearyall, but for the most part the red-roofed houses cluster about the churches of St John and St Benedict. The mighty abbey is somehow walled off from the gaze of the watching Tor by the shoulder of Chalice Hill, as if the mysteries of each are kept out of sight of the other. The tower on the summit is that of a chapel dedicated to St Michael, the great archangel who overcame the Evil One. That is another thread in the skein of history and myth of this place. The chapel itself fell down in an earthquake long ago, yet its tall tower stands untouched. Legend, to some extent supported by archaeological evidence, tells us that before the chapel there was a circle of standing stones on the Tor's crest.

From earliest times Glastonbury has always been a place to go to as part of a spiritual pilgrimage, perhaps to visit a shrine dedicated to the worship of the sun on the Tor, or in more recent times to attend the Glastonbury fair, held in 1971. This was originally intended as a Pop Festival held at Pilton, a few miles away, but somehow it became something else. Many of the large numbers of folk who attended recall it, even now, as an experience of spiritual moment. Certainly the Christian pilgrims of earlier years often wrote of the effect the place had on them. Its mystique is still very apparent to some; to others Glastonbury is just a small West Country town with a ruined abbey, a few gift shops, and, if you know where to go, pubs selling local rough and potent cider.

The earliest settlers of the area were fishers and fowlers in a marsh where pelicans flew in warmer ages, nearly 3,000 years ago. The folk of Meare and Godney were predominantly bronze

Glastonbury. The ridged Tor, crowned with St Michael's chapel tower, looms over the Abbey ruins and the town's clustering houses. (*Aerofilms*)

users, and they were skilled in the working of this metal into the agricultural tools used on the drier uplands around the edges of the mere. They also fashioned 'La Tène'-type brooches, antique forerunners of the modern safety-pin, which were used to fasten their woven cloaks and tunics in place. Loom weights have been found, so no doubt local wool was woven into cloth, perhaps of the simple checked or tartan pattern which seems to have been popular in the Bronze Age Celtic settlements. Iron was also worked, and pottery, much made without the wheel, has been found in the area. This is often elaborately decorated with the whorls and scrolls of those half-animal, half-abstract designs which are so typical of the Celtic art form, and which have often been discovered here. The Glastonbury Bowl of this period is decorated with knobs like a riveted copper dish. Boats have been found, constructed from great logs, carefully hollowed by fire and adze, from which the lake dwellers would have caught fish and wildfowl. Their main hunting weapon seems to have been the slingshot, and many hardened clay bullets have been discovered in the marsh.

Behind their palisades, in round huts with clay hearths, these folk may have lived peacefully for quite some time, for the hearths have been found one above the other during excavations, but at some time there was an attack from some early invaders who burned their way west to Godney. In the beginning of the Christian era these Belgae destroyed one lake village, but the other survived, though it never grew or flourished artistically as previously. Maybe many of its people had perished in the Belgic invasion, and only a few survivors continued to live in the reed-surrounded islands.

Many seasons passed over this summer land of Somerset, but always, within the shadow of England's natural pyramid of the Tor, people came and went through this land of legend. The Romans crossed the area to visit the lead mines in the Mendips. There was probably a harbour or landing stage built out over the marshes at Ponter's Ball, and maybe the strange ships from Phoenicia called here on their merchant-venturing journeys in search of precious metals and items of trade. Even that place later to be called the Holy Land sent its traders here for tin and lead and hides. Certainly the jetty was there in the Iron Age.

Legend has it that after the Crucifixion Joseph of Arimathea travelled west in search of rest and contemplation, and that with a few followers he roved until at last, tired of journeying, he came ashore on a green bank, and to mark his arrival, planted his thorny staff into the ground. It gave forth leaves and blossoms, and even now we can watch the strange occurrence of a thorn tree blossoming not only in early summer, but in the depths of winter. It is certainly not the common hawthorn of Britain, being more of a tree than the well-known hedge shrub of southern counties. *Crataegus aronia* is certainly a variety found in Asia, around Jerusalem, and on the Mount of Olives where traditionally preserves have been made of its fruit. Hawthorn wood is often used for staffs and shepherds' crooks where its size and shape are suitable; it is also the hottest burning wood on a fire.

On Wearyall Hill beside Glastonbury town, above the lapping marsh waters, the original thorn tree grew and blossomed twice a year, and many pilgrims visiting the ancient Christian shrines at

A fine example of the Holy Thorn which flowers on Old Christmas Day as well as late spring, outside St John's Church, Glastonbury. (*British Tourist Authority*)

Glastonbury may have seen it and taken leaves or cuttings as souvenirs. Few of these offspring of the old tree survived, which helped to prove that it was not natural to these shores. This tree on the hill flourished with its double trunk and winter flowers until the reign of Elizabeth I, when a Protestant zealot attacked it with an axe, felling one part. However, on chopping at the second stem – so legend has it – the axe rebounded, striking his leg, and a chip of wood hit him in the eye, partially blinding him. After this he left the rest of the tree alone. It was finally struck down during the Civil War, but luckily for us today, not before cuttings had been successfully struck in the area, so that even now this little tree which symbolises the return of the Light in midwinter can be seen, replaced near its original position on Wearyall Hill. Because of the change in the calendar the white blossoms can be seen in early January when all our native hawthorns are black and bare.

Travellers took sprigs of the tree with them for luck, and Queen Anne was presented with a spray of the flowers. Since 1929 the reigning monarch has also received this gift of hawthorn at the New Year. Some have considered that the thorns were the sort used to crown Jesus at the Crucifixion; others say that it is blossoming at Yuletide to welcome the birth of the Saviour. Either way, it is a pleasing sight, these delicate white flowers with their golden/pink centres and heady, musky scent. Kipling wrote:

> You'll go where laurel crowns are won, but will you e'er
>   forget
> The smell of hawthorn in the sun, and bracken in the wet?

Glastonbury is still a shrine as it was from the very beginning of the Christian era. The history of the abbey, of which so little remains standing today, is varied and mysterious. Since its last destruction in the Dissolution of the Monasteries in 1539, its mighty walls have been quarried by the local folk, and many a cottage and barn stands mute witness to that great construction of stone; here and there a carven face or foliate capital has been incorporated in a humbler building in the locality. Of the actual abbey ruins, none is older than about 1185, for a serious fire broke out in May 1184 and the whole abbey was consumed except for a small portion, including the Bell Tower which remained standing. The monks were left only a room or two in which to dwell. This was a great secular and spiritual loss, for the church contained not only beautiful and valuable silver and gold plate, but a great library and the relics of a number of saints which were consumed in the conflagration.

Legend tells us that the old church on the site of the later abbey, within the still-standing walls, was a small wattle chapel built by the followers of Christ themselves, within a few years of His departure from among them. This foundation was apparently dedicated and in use by folk who must have been among the earliest Christians outside the Holy Land. Certainly the place was sanctified and well established before the fifth century, as William of Malmesbury, who wrote the history of the abbey, tells us that St Patrick visited the place, and his death is put in A.D. 461. A number of other saints and important figures have their stories woven into the overall legends of the place.

Even before the coming of the first Christians the strange hill above the low swamp-lands must have attracted visitors. There is some archaeological evidence that a ring of standing stones was at the top of the Tor before the first of the later chapels was placed there. Many early Celtic shrines were found on high, isolated hilltops, or near ever-running sacred springs. Glastonbury has both, for close to the Tor is the 'blood-spring', Chalice Well, on the side of the hill just across the valley. Here the water runs clear and sparkling come rain or drought, and where the water wells up in the deep stone chamber of the present spring, a water fungus forms blood-red coagulations near the surface, due perhaps to the salts and iron in the water. It is pleasant and cool to drink, without the bitter mineral taste of some spa waters, and has a reputation for healing. Now the well is in the gardens laid out by the Chalice Well Trust, and visitors may stroll among neat beds of herbs and sweet-smelling flowers, or dally on the smooth-shaven lawns around the gushing lion-head fountain where glasses may be filled to sample the water. The modern lid which covers the well-head is decorated with interlinked circles of mystical significance, and around the well there is a pavement of stones, many with large ammonites, from the local quarries. On a hot summer's day it is hard to find a more pleasant pursuit, especially after climbing the steep Tor, than pausing among fragrant herbs and tasting water unaffected by chemicals, other than those which Nature provides (and thus somewhat strange to our chemical-additive-familiar palates). As you drink it is well to remember the other pilgrims who, possibly for thousands of

The modern lid covering the ancient 'blood spring', the ever-running waters of Chalice Well at Glastonbury.

years, have quenched their thirst of these selfsame waters, and quietly give thanks for sacred well-springs, running free. Beneath the abbey undercroft there is another, darker well, like Lethe to Chalice's Nemosthene. St Joseph's well is dimly seen behind a grille of iron under a Norman arch in the abbey ruins, its water reflecting bluish in torchlight, but it does not have the life-giving appeal of the blood-red spring on the hillside above. To reach St Joseph's well there is a strange, steep stair with uneven steps to help monks with filled buckets toiling from the spring to the kitchens, or about their chores. Try climbing these to see how difficult it must have been to lug pails without spilling their contents.

The Tor hill has many legends, but to continue the story of the abbey, we find it well established by the time of the Saxon invasions and the days of King Arthur, *circa* sixth century. Here is another strand of the many aspects of our history and legends which are drawn from all parts of Christendom, yet here at Glastonbury, woven into a tapestry of ancient design, on which it is possible still to discern the picture which has been created about the fields of Avalon. The Arthurian thread is woven into the abbey's story. The myth of Arthur depicts him as the undying king, wounded at the battle of Camlann by Mordred, his bastard son, then carried west in a boat by three dark queens to Avalon, to be healed of his wounds and await the summons to return. In the legend he is still waiting, but in the history of Somerset Arthur has a real place. He was probably a war leader who led the Britons against the Saxon invaders in the sixth century. Excavations at Cadbury Castle have shown that the place was re-fortified in Arthur's time. (This is another weird site to visit on a misty summer evening, when the wind whispers in the trees that throng the ditches of the great embankments, sounding like horses galloping.) Certainly there is evidence of a battle, and this large hill-fort would make an ideal place of relative safety where the folk and the livestock could be gathered, and from its heights a lookout over the surrounding landscape could be kept. Forays from the well-defended gateway could be made to oppose invading forces, and from the lofty walls, probably palisaded with wooden posts, slingshots and arrows could be poured upon the enemy below.

According to Giraldus Cambrensis, writing about 1190, Arthur's last journey was to Avalon, and the monks who made excavations after the great fire in 1184 discovered the grave of a Celtic chieftain, containing the skeletons of a tall man and a fair woman; Arthur and Guinevere? This was a further draw to pilgrims, and historians have argued whether it was a put-up job, a sort of medieval publicity stunt to attract more visitors and thus more income to the abbey, which desperately needed additions to its rebuilding fund. There is the famous lead cross supposed to have come from the grave of Arthur, with its Latin inscription: *Hic jacet sepultus inclitus Rex Arturius in insula Avalonia.* Various versions of this inscription have been given by different historians, including one translated as: 'Here lies the body of Arthur, King that was and King that is yet to be' – hence the title of T. H. White's book, *The Once and Future King.* The monks may have found bones in a grave which closely resembled those of Celtic persons of note, and in a part of the graveyard of the abbey where nobles would have been interred. This may account for the historical *Dux Bellorum,* the war leader, but it does not necessarily wipe out the legend of the king who sleeps, surrounded by his knights and destined to rise up to defend the homeland in the last great battle. The Welsh bard wrote: 'ANOETH BID BET Y ARTHUR' – variously interpreted but generally implying: 'A mystery to the world is the grave of Arthur', and that it is unwise to enquire about this mystery.

Yet another thread of this complex pattern is that of the Holy Grail. In the Christian tradition the Grail is thought to be either the vessel that Jesus drank from at the Last Supper, or some kind of cup in which Joseph of Arimathea collected the sweat and blood of the dying Christ on the cross. According to another of the Glastonbury legends the Grail was brought there by Joseph and hidden in the chamber of Chalice Well, hence both its name, Chalice, and also why it is the blood-spring with red-tinged waters. This strand of myth links up with King Arthur and his knights whose quest for the Holy Grail gave a spiritual impetus to this otherwise rather warlike band. There are many interpretations of the Grail; in some it is simply a cup sacred in the Christian tradition for its association with the passion of Jesus, but in the Arthurian tales there are older fragments which take its history back long before the Christian era. In the Welsh mythology there was a magical cauldron in which the sorceress/Goddess Cerridwen brewed a potion to grant wisdom to her son, who had no natural virtues. Her plans went astray, but it seems the cauldron became accounted among the Treasures of Britain. This magic cooking-pot was variously attributed with the power of restoring life to those slain in battle, after their bodies had been cast into it; it also cooked the favourite meal for any man who dared to eat from it. The Welsh stories have Arthur seeking it in the Celtic otherworld, Annwn, which perhaps relates to Avalon.

Always there seem to be twin strands woven into the pattern. There is the thread of historical truth which modern methods of archaeology are in many cases strengthening, and there is the more subtle thread of myth, often spun of many varied fibres drawn from local tradition, ancient folk tales which form archetypal patterns behind the hero or event under consideration. There are many stories of undying heroes who have to face great odds to recover strange treasures from distant lands, or from the underworld/otherworld. These occur in the mythology of many lands, and so often the successful quester sails off into the sunset to rest until his skill is needed again. With Arthur, the results of the dig begun at Cadbury Castle in 1966 have confirmed many of the historical details of his time. There were Saxon invasions in the sixth century; Cadbury Castle, a large Iron Age hill-fort, was re-fortified at that time, and there is evidence of a battle in the vicinity. Perhaps it is not the Camelot of the musical, with its glittering towers, ladies in incredible medieval head-dresses and velvet gowns strolling among virile, armoured knights who were prepared to joust for their favours. It certainly is a stronghold, and to the simple peasant folk who were harboured within its quadruple banks and ditches for security, it must have seemed like a vast and teeming city.

Today the stories of Arthur, like the Biblical tales derived from the Coventry and Wakefield cycles of mystery plays, are re-enacted at the site of the abbey which may well have witnessed some parts of the real events. The monks of the abbey may even have acted out the older versions of these sacred/secular stories whereby the events of the Church's calendar were played out in church before the congregation. Later the members of the different craft guilds took the simple plays to the folk by acting in the streets on moving stages of carts and wagons.

The Grail, too, has not been forgotten. It has influenced the works of many writers, poets, playwrights, musicians and opera composers, as well as psychologists and thinkers, ever since the Middle Ages. The question, 'Whom does the Grail serve?' may have been solved many times – or never. To T. S. Eliot 'The Wasteland' is still real, the Fisher King still maimed and his country lying barren and unfruitful. It is easy to imagine the lame king in his cold castle above the mirroring mere, awaiting with infinite patience the seeker who would have the right question and the right answer to restore his powers and bring back fertility to the empty lands. Does he still ponder, invisible, on Wearyall Hill where the road called Fisher's Hill climbs the whaleback shape? Here is another strand of the weaving, and another enigma for the magical mystery tour of Glastonbury.

As if there were not already enough puzzles for this quiet Somerset town where distant myth intersects with real history and flows forwards to the present day, there is the matter of the Glastonbury Zodiac. If you can't accept some of the myths attached to this place, and you have actually been within its magical, mystical atmosphere, then these tales will remain within the realms of faerie. But . . . if something of its strangeness has gripped you, if something of its otherworldly nature has struck chords in your heart or imagination, then consider this: A circle of figures representing the signs of the Zodiac 10 miles across, symbolic figures which also fit into the stories of King Arthur, the great circle, 30 miles in circumference, itself being the Round Table which would seat a multitude, and all of it designed and laid out with rivers, hills, pathways and field-boundaries, something like 3,500 years ago; each sign also happening to fall into the correct place if the stars of the constellations are projected on to them on the relevant scale. Impossible? Unlikely? Incredible? All these may be thoughts which rush through your mind at the very idea, yet archaeology and computer science have combined to try to explain the positioning of the megaliths of Stonehenge and Callanish which relate to specific positions of sun and moon with incredible accuracy.

In 1925 Katherine Maltwood was working on illustrations for the *High History of the Holy Grail,* which may well have originated from the pen of a monk at Glastonbury, written in Norman-French, for many of the locations are recognisable even today. As she tried to map out the area of the Grail Quests she suddenly noticed the very figures of the tale staring out of the flat surface of the map before her astonished eyes. The first to emerge was Leo, the great lion, rampant, drawn in part by the River Cary and partly by an ancient trackway, Somerton Lane. His tangled mane is drawn by woods, marked on the map as Catsash Hundred. Towards the villages of Compton and Dundon there are rambling hills, wooded and overgrown, but from the air the ancient earthworks and natural shapes of the land seem to depict a huge child, curled like an unborn baby, with one arm arching over its head, slumping towards Lollover Hill. Mrs Maltwood managed to obtain aerial photographs of the whole area and gradually, working with these and with 6-inch O.S. maps which give old field names, tracks, rivers and streams, she uncovered a whole series of figures, often several miles across. These fit not only into the stories of King Arthur and his knights, but also represent versions of the ancient signs of the Zodiac, each lying on the ground to mirror the stars in the constellations above. A coincidence? Maybe – but there are local legends of a lion and a giant in the Vale of Avalon.

Each of the twelve zodiacal signs is represented in its proper place by a figure or symbol which fits in with the traditions of astrology. True, some of the forms used are not those we see today in the astrology column of the daily Press, but there is plenty of old evidence that some of the modern signs have older counterparts. Here is some of the evidence which supports the existence of these huge figures; perhaps it will interest others to research the legends, or get out the maps and look for other signs.

Aries the Ram, kneeling like the paschal lamb, is drawn by trackways across the sheep-rearing and shearing area to the west of Glastonbury. In the Arthurian cycle he has been compared with the rash Gawain who would fight best in the morning, because his strength waned after noon. He is the first sign of the Zodiac, and also the first in the Grail Quest. 'Mares eat oats and does eat oats, but little lambs eat ivy . . .' goes the old song, and Ivythorn Hill helps to outline this sacrificial lamb, where the local youth hostel is situated!

Taurus the Bull – or at least part-bull – of the Zodiac is also partly drawn by Ivythorn Hill, and Collard Hill is on his neck. His eye used to be marked by a dewpond where cattle were watered, and there was a rifle-range nearby. The Pleiades, that faint group of stars within Taurus, fall at the top of Collard Hill, where some coincidence has caused the erection of a tall obelisk, the Hood Memorial, which makes a very fine horn for this bull. Taurus is associated with Sir Ector, Arthur's guardian, who was stolid and home-loving, though capable of fighting, as will any bull, when roused.

Next in the Zodiac are those terrible twins of Gemini, here represented by the baby on Dundon Hill. In the church at Compton Dundon (twin villages on these signs) are several fascinating roof bosses, including a charming dragon, picked out in red and green, towards the altar, and a fine foliate head peers down at worshippers in this tiny, delightful church. There is the head of an angel watching from the top of a window, a small surviving fragment of old glass, and a finely carved pulpit is set halfway through the thick walls. The pews have narrow and extremely uncomfortable kneeling benches where most churches have rests for hymn books. It is just possible to kneel on them balanced upright!

The High History of the Holy Grail, which has some decidedly weird versions of the Arthurian tales, links in older stories of the Sun God, who is doomed to die each cycle as the sun in the sky fades with each passing year. Arthur is one aspect of the sun, and his bastard son is another. Each threatens death to the other, their fates inextricably entwined from the start, for there cannot be two suns in one sky. If you look at a map of this area it is not difficult to see another face here, the woods and earthworks of Dundon Hill outlining the lineaments of a face so like the traditional crucified Christ, slumping over in death or weariness. Perhaps this is a grown twin, Galahad of Arthur's Round Table, who sought the Grail with determination and bravery for he had already sat in Siege Perilous, the strange seat fashioned by Merlin. Or is this uncomfortable and dangerous throne the next sign of the Zodiac – Cancer?

Usually this symbol is the Crab, scuttling sideways through the sky, the summer stars of the summer land, but here in the most watery area of the Zodiac, for it is low down on the marshes, there is a great ship. Within this the figure of the baby floats, like Moses and many another sun hero in a basket/boat. Whereas many of the figures are outlined by trackways and the natural hill shapes, this boat is drawn by canals and streams. It has been said that these waterways are fairly recent, in historical terms, and astronomical evidence sets this Zodiac in extremely ancient times, but there may well have been older streams which formed the shape, or it may have differed in the past. Certainly it is one of the easiest signs to pick out of the new metric O.S. maps of the area. Arthur was concerned with boats at various times in his career, rowing with Merlin to take Excalibur from the hand of the Lady of the Lake, and after his final battle, sailing in that barge of glass with the three dark queens, or pre-Christian goddesses, to the Isle of Apples. At the prow of the boat the map shows Lugshorn; Lug is Lugh or Llew the Sun God, the figurehead of this moon-crescent boat. This craft is the most westerly of the Zodiac signs, too, and there are many tales of heroes sailing into the sunset, to rest and await their summons to return. Has Arthur, that inspiration and archetype of king/hero, sailed away to some unseen land beyond the sunset, gone to await his recall when his native land needs him, as it did in the days of the Saxon invaders? Has he linked up with another ancient British custom, with St George in the Padstow 'Obby 'Oss May Day song?

> Where is St George, where is he, O?
> He's out in his long boat, all on the salt sea, O.

The Padstow 'Oss could easily have started its life as a coracle.

Leo, Mrs Maltwood's first figure comes next, the most southerly figure, and one of the largest. A great west-facing lion sprawls across the countryside with places like Catsash, Catsgore and Catsham scattered around him. He is probably Lancelot, that lion-like knight who was undefeated, yet who betrayed his king by allying himself with Guinevere, playing a cat and mouse game with his liege lord. On the land of Leo there is an alabaster quarry as well as the remains of various Roman villas. Joseph of Arimathea is supposed to have been buried in a place of red earth and white stones, and this is just what the quarry is like. Even today it is possible to extract pieces of this fascinating soft rock from the sides of the old workings where it forms bright layers in the reddish stone like the inside of the caves at nearby Wookey Hole, with stalagmites and crystalline forms.

Virgo, the lady of the Zodiac, must be Guinevere, but here she is aspects of all the pagan goddesses as well as the Virgin Mary. Drawn by the River Cary, who as Mother Cary, or Ceres, has many chickens, as the sea birds are often called, she offers a bunch of flowers or a sheaf of corn with her outstretched hand, for Virgo is an Earth sign. Her bosom covers the fields, and Wimble Toot, or teat, is an artificial tumulus on her nipple. Virgin she may be, but her fat belly lies on the village of Babcary. Legend has it that the village is easy to get into, but difficult to get out of! Virgo reaches out towards the villages of Charlton Adam, that early gardener, and Charlton Mackrell, harking back to the Sea Goddess and the harvest of the sea. Annis Hill relates to the old hag who ties in with Cerridwen, the third aspect to the Moon Goddess of Celtic times, for this figure has two faces: an old granny (St Anne was Jesus's grandmother), and the young maiden, with eyes made up of ponds, glittering blue under a summer sky. Above her head, near Downhead (Virgo is almost upside down), is Stockwitch Cross, showing the treacherous side of Guinevere, who betrayed her husband with his best friend. Or perhaps this is a reference, nearby, to Arthur's witch sister, Morgan le Fay.

Libra too has reverted to an older version of its sign, and from the scales of justice becomes the dove of peace, diving to Barton St David. 'Dafydd' – which is the Welsh version of the name as distinct from the Hebrew – is a form of the word 'dove', and this bird seems to speed downwards to the heart of the Zodiac, via Hurtle Pool. Its outspread wings seem to refer to the Grail and its appearance within Grail Castle before the Four Hallows, or holy things. Above it is Silver Street – the glow above the shining cup, perhaps.

Overleaf An Ordnance Survey map of the area south of Glastonbury showing the signs of the Zodiac which Katherine Maltwood identified in 1925.

THE GREAT DOG OF LANGPORT
CANCER
Westhay
Meare
Meare Heath
Shapwick Heath
Edington Heath
Catcott Heath
Nidons
Cossington
Chilton Polden
Edington
Catcott
Stawell
Shapwick
Ashcott
Moorlinch
Sutton Mallet
Greinton
Pedwell
Walton
Street
Westonzoyland
King's Sedge Moor
Butleigh Moor
Middlezoy
Othery
Greylake
Henley
High Ham
Beer
Aller
Low Ham
Burrow Bridge
Southlake Moor
North Moor
Langport
Huish Episcopi
Pitney
Wagg
Upton
Curry Rivel
Drayton
Muchelney
West Sedge Moor
Somerton Door
Long Load

CAPRICORN
AQUARIUS
SAGITTARIUS
SCORPIO
LIBRA
LEO
VIRGO
North Wootton
Pilton
West Pennard
East Pennard
West Bradley
Baltonsborough
Butleigh
Compton Dundon
Kingweston
Barton St David
Keinton Mandeville
Lovington
Somerton
Charlton Mackrell
Charlton Adam
Babcary
Kingsdon
Podimore
West Camel
Queen Camel
Queen's Sedge Moor
South Moor
Kennard Moor
Pilton Park
Ham Street
West Lydford
East Lydford
Cary Fitzpaine
Yeovilton Airfield

Scorpio seems to represent the darker aspect of the Arthurian legend – Mordred, Arthur's bastard/incestuous son, whose efforts to destroy the king led to his own downfall, as the scorpion stings itself to death sometimes. In astrology Scorpio is the eighth house which is concerned with death and secrecy, and this sign is well hidden, between the main figures of Guinevere in Virgo, and Arthur, the mounted knight, in Sagittarius. Lottisham is on Scorpio, and Lot, King of the Orkneys, was supposed to have plotted against Arthur, in league, according to some stories, with Morgan le Fay.

The Sagittarius figure in this Zodiac gets over the compound Archer/Horse symbol by depicting a knight, his arm drawn back as if pulling a bow, being flung from his staggering horse towards the centre of this great wheel. Again we find village names giving some substance to the legend, for Canters Green and Breech Lane are on the hind quarters of the figure, and Arthur's Bridge nearby. We have another link between Arthur and St George, both knights who fought dragons, for here Arthur tackles the great figure of Scorpio on one side, and a huge fish on the other. King's Hill is marked here, too.

Capricorn, the sea-goat, is taken to be the wise Merlin, that shadowy figure who hovers in the background of the Arthurian myth, from Arthur's omened birth, perhaps at Tintagel in Cornwall, to his final confrontation with Mordred at Camlann. Here Capricorn has a single horn, the Iron Age jetty in the marshes at Ponter's Ball. Perhaps he is the unicorn to match the Lion of Lancelot, thus supporting Arthur as he always did. Merlin was said to be a Druid, and there are two ancient oak trees, known as the Druid Oaks, or Gog and Magog, below the Tor, towards which this unicorn is reaching, to graze on its green slopes.

Glastonbury town is in the sign of Aquarius, the symbol of the dawning of the New Age. Aquarius is the Water Bearer, and there have always been sparkling special wells in the area, and the still meres. No man with a water-pot is shown here, but the older sign of the Phoenix – he who is reborn from his own ashes. Again the coincidence of place names comes into play. The Phoenix builds a nest of spices which becomes his funeral pyre, and at the bottom of Glastonbury is Cinnamon Lane. Strip lynchets form the feathers on his upraised wings which show quite clearly in aerial photographs.

Glastonbury is a place in transition, for although the main

layout of the town and the abbey and its eternal hills is little changed by time nor even by modern traffic, the subtle atmosphere of the place has gone through a number of stages. When the first recent Glastonbury Festival was held in 1971 there was a terrific outcry against the 'hippies' who flocked to the place for the music and 'vibes'. Many shops sprouted notices declaring 'No Hippies Served', although I don't think the genus 'hippie' was ever clearly defined. It seemed in practice to cover anyone, of either sex, wearing jeans and long hair, beads and a happy smile. This prohibition has finally faded from the last of the pubs only recently and the tattered notices have at last been removed. Glastonbury has been the beginning of many a trend; it has been the setting for a play on television about the birth of the new Messiah, it has been considered the ancient Avalon, and also the new Jerusalem – Blake's familiar words of the hymn could so easily refer to these 'pastures seen . . . and was Jerusalem builded here, among those dark, Satanic mills?' Anyone who has seen a thunderstorm building up above Wells or Priddy, will see how that is true.

The last sign in this terrestrial Zodiac is that of Pisces, the symbol which was associated with Christ's ministry, when He made His disciples 'Fishers of Men'. Here the fishes of the symbol are represented by two small fish shapes drawn beneath the head of Taurus, beside the great whale-back hump of Wearyall Hill which resembles a surfacing leviathan above the marshy lowlands. What is intriguing is that the abbey, that very foundation of Christianity in this land, lies nestled between the two fish. Joseph, that intrepid traveller from the East landed, we are to believe, on Wearyall Hill, thus founding the faith of the Piscean Age upon the whale (which, in his time, was probably regarded as a fish rather than as a marine mammal). In Arthur's story perhaps this was the location of the castle of the maimed Fisher King, who guarded the Grail yet could not use its healing and revitalising power until another came to answer the question: 'Whom does the Grail serve?' He waited, impotent, in his dark castle as various of the Grail Knights on their initiatory quest found him and witnessed the appearance of the Grail Hallows, guarded by maidens, yet ever veiled and unreachable. Only the pure in spirit could come to the Grail face to face. Was the modern Pomparles Bridge the actual 'Pons Perilous'? Yet another coincidence in this weird place, where Carl Jung's theories of 'Synchronicity' must have *some* meaning.

Another interpretation of this huge circular plan of the Zodiac signs is that this is in fact King Arthur's Round Table which would seat a multitude, or that it is itself the Grail, cupped by living hills, filled with the pure waters of the holy springs, the third of which has sadly been buried under a trading estate at Beckery. The blood-red spring rises in its heart, supplying the water mingled with the red of wine; above it seems to hang a halo of brightness when clouds are low, apparently supported by the tower of St Michael on the Tor. Beneath such clouds radiance shines all round the horizon, reflecting gleams from the not-so-distant sea, beyond Brent Knoll.

Even now we have not come to the end of the mysteries of Glastonbury. On the Tor is the pattern of what might so easily be a maze path copying the sacred sevenfold design drawn upon the floor of Chartres Cathedral, traced on ancient Cretan coins, inscribed on rocks by Red Indian shamans. Again from the air this maze can be seen, making some sense of the ridges and pathways which wind back and forth around the steep sides of the Tor, yet by being followed on foot are themselves never steep. Erosion has flattened some parts; cattle and men, walking the ridgeback way from the town and Wellhouse Lane, have cut across the interwoven, twisting way of the maze, but parts are still clearly visible, and not really likely to be mere cattle paths on this most uncanny hill.

If you draw a straight line on a map from St Michael's Mount in Cornwall to Glastonbury's Michael-Tower on the Tor and onwards, you will find it continues through Avebury, that largest and most ancient monument to the ingenuity of our remote ancestors. Continued, this line crosses the whole country to go over the edge near Bury St Edmunds. On the southern side this line, known to some as the Great Dragon Line, passes over the churches dedicated to Michael, that mighty archangel on Brentor, also the ruined chapel forming the nose of another vast earth creature, the Questing Beast, at St Michael's on Burrowbridge Mump. Churches dedicated to SS Michael and George abound on this line; both were concerned with overcoming dragons or devils, both are closely associated with the festivals, appearing in folk plays, being celebrated in ceremonial songs, or as the Light that overcomes the darkness, being remembered in bonfires and torchlight. Many ancient sites are to be found on similar straight lines, too many to be sheer coincidence, and the tracing of these has become the fairly new

The banners of the Anglican pilgrims are paraded up the High Street towards the Abbey in June each year. (*Brian Walker*)

hobby of ley-hunting. Interest in this phenomenon was first quickened when *The Old Straight Track,* written by the late Alfred Watkins of Hereford, was published in 1925, and the investigations of recent years have been encouraged by Paul Screeton, author of *Quicksilver Heritage.* That is another story!

What, you may ask, has all this got to do with a festival at Glastonbury? Actually it is the reason for there being any sort of celebration there at all. The plays in the abbey, revived in 1969 under the title *Miracles at Glastonbury,* draw together some of the threads of this complex tapestry which I have tried to explain. There have been many miracles at Glastonbury, healings and hauntings, the coming of significant people such as Joseph and, some say, even Jesus, either as a child or after the Crucifixion. Arthur in history and legend has been associated with this place, and perhaps his mortal remains were buried within the abbey's sacred precincts. Still they come, the Anglican pilgrims at the end of June, the new pilgrims who seek inspiration for new music, new poetry, new ways of living, at midsummer. Glastonbury has inspired many, and the earlier festivals of music and poetry at the Assembly Rooms, now being restored for similar use, gave birth to the works of Rutland Boughton, whose *Immortal Hour* is but a fragment of a work inspired by Glastonbury. John Cowper Powys's *A Glastonbury Romance,* which must surely be one of the thickest paperbacks in print, springs from here; the occultist and psychologist Dion Fortune lived on the Tor, and wrote many of her books, including *The Cosmic Doctrine,* a treatise on the past and future of the spirit of Man, under the spell of the place. Geoffrey Ashe, that learned Arthurian scholar, Christian thinker, and patron of Glastonbury's heritage, has set his first novel, *The Finger and the Moon,* in this uncanny landscape.

When the ruins of the abbey were being excavated in the first couple of decades of this century, Frederick Bligh Bond, who was in charge, recovered several forgotten chapels. Obvious, you may say, although the standing masonry gave few clues, and written records hinted rather than explained, that chapels would be found around such a holy place. It was only the intervention of one of the monks, communicating across the centuries by means of automatic writing to one of Bligh Bond's friends, that led to the discovery of the Edgar Chapel to the east of the existing church, and later the Loretto Chapel. In each case extremely detailed information directed the diggers; it was given by several communicators, partly in Latin, partly in the English of St Dunstan's time. The colour of the glass in the windows, the shapes of the walls and the dimensions of the buildings were all given, and later research confirmed the accuracy of the scripts.

In the time of Elizabeth I, her astrologer Dr John Dee and his associate Edward Kelly came to Glastonbury, guided by an ancient manuscript which led them to find, in a grave in St Benignus's (St Benedict's) churchyard, two small phials of powder, one red, one white (which, though harking back to the blood and sweat of Christ, and Joseph's Grail, in this case were concerned with alchemy). Using some of these chemical substances, legend has it that Dee managed to transmute part of a copper warming-pan into alchemical gold. Another of Glastonbury's miracles? Well, there is an alchemist's knife in the Natural History Museum in London, in the geological section – and the bottom part of the steel blade is gold!

So, if you happen to be in Somerset during the summer, when the various festivals are held, or in the winter when the Holy

Thorn flowers (there is a fine specimen in St John's churchyard), or if you are in the area simply because some inner urge calls you there – then take the road that runs down from the hills, across the plain, perhaps on one of the ways engineered in the Bronze Age, to where the Tor hunches up from the flat landscape, and enter this land where myth and history join. If you come in spring to Avalon, the Isle of Apples, whose crooked trees lean on the feet of the Tor, snowing its lower slopes with pale pink blossom, remember it was with the Silver Branch that Bran, the Sun God (who became Michael in the Christian era), gained entry and safe return from the Otherworld. Remember, too, if you discover which of the pubs sells real cider, not fizzy yellow stuff in bottles but honey-coloured liquid sunlight as seen through the mists of this land, you are drinking the wine of heroes, that which restores life and bestows wisdom, for it is the juice of the fruit of the Tree of Knowledge. It is also very potent if you are not used to its sweet yet sharp taste!

And if you come soon you may be in at the next miracle, when Glastonbury's Phoenix rises from its ashes to greet the Aquarian Age. . . .

CHAPTER 4

Six Men and a fool dance in the Thaxted Ring

Now ladies and gentlemen who sit by the fire,
Put your hands in your pockets, that's all we desire,
Put your hand in your pocket and pull out your purse,
And give us a trifle, you won't feel much worse . . .

Trad. children's rhyme

Ever since I was a small child the chink and jingle of Morris bells, the thud of the dancers' feet and clash of their sticks, accompanied by fiddle or accordion music attenuated by being outdoors, has fascinated me. It drew me to watch the Morris dancers beside the Thames, outside a towpath pub in my home town, or stand enthralled when they danced on the village greens of Kent and Sussex, when I was visiting various relatives in those parts. Always men, always dressed in white and bright ribbons, or colourful waistcoats curiously decorated with trees, ships, faces, and all manner of traditional symbols. They were most often seen in summer, dancing outside certain public houses, or occasionally at garden fêtes, or taking part in some local procession of decorated floats, dancing along the road, between the motorised lorries.

It wasn't until I started to travel around the South of England and take notice of the differing attire of Morris Men, the variety of their instruments and tunes to which they danced, that I realised this was something other than a local pastime of a few groups of enthusiasts. It was about then that I heard a friend, Brian Peacock, talking about Morris Dancing in a way that showed he knew what it was about. He admitted that he had danced himself, and said that if I was keen on the activity I ought to attend a Morris Ring meeting. 'What is a Ring, then?' – I enquired, and it was explained to me that every so often whole contingents of Morris teams or sides gathered in one place for a day's dancing, ale or cider drinking, singing, and any other country pursuit which occurred to them. The most famous was that held at Thaxted, a small village in Essex, a place rather off my normal beat, and well worth the effort of getting there.

Nothing much happened for a time, but then I received one of Brian's entertaining and informative letters, hinting that the time for the Thaxted meeting was drawing near and that he intended to go. He had written with some of the background information to spur me on, and included a book, *Thaxted Quest for Social Justice,* subtitled *Autobiography of a Turbulent Priest and Rebel,* by Rev. Jack Putterill, who was so involved with the folk, their dances and well-being. It was he who encouraged the Morris Men. With Brian's permission, I quote from his communication at length:

> I come not from Heaven, but from Essex . . .
>
> East Anglia is flat. Everyone knows that, especially those who have never walked or cycled there. There are, however, only two main roads into the region, one to the South and the other to the West; this is because the whole area is cut off from the rest of the country by the marshes of the Fens to the north-west, the Essex marshes to the south-east, and a line of low but nasty, bumpy hills across Essex to Cambridge.
>
> You might, though, at a whim, ignore the main A11 road and penetrate the local road running along the next valley – the valley of the little River Roding. You would pass old Essex villages with quaint names – Chipping Ongar, Fyfield, Bacon End, and the seven Rodings: Abess, Aythorpe, Beauchamp, High, Leaden, Margaret, and White! Through Dunmow, of flitch fame, you would go; passing the gigantic bacon factory (of course, the only possible industry in this town!)
>
> Eventually you would get to Saffron Walden, the bustling market town named for the Saffron Crocus grown there long ago to colour and spice Old English cooking. Who said curry came from India? Proper English mincemeat is just a good fruity, curried mince (nothing at all like that made and sold today); so was Christmas Plum Porridge.
>
> But I digress. If you have got to Saffron you have already passed, by 10 miles, the place I'm supposed to be talking about. Yes, it's tiny enough, called a town and was one once, during its prosperity, lying in a sudden hollow in the bumpy

Essex plain. If it wasn't for the bend in the main street and the two sharp turns at the top, you wouldn't even have slowed down.

Nevertheless, you did slow down, because you had to! The road from London leads straight down the hill at a half-timbered building with a completely open ground floor, the Moot Hall. Behind it is a most enormous church, like all those in East Anglia far too big for the town. Its spire sticks up out of the hollow to dominate all the surrounding countryside. These two buildings, plus some fine Queen Anne/Tudor houses are really the whole town, if you discount the sweet factory and the new estates. This is the once extremely prosperous wool centre of Thaxted. The vast church, like many in the region, was built on the profits of wool. Few expensive men are needed to keep sheep, and only a few well-placed landowners are needed to force through Acts of Parliament compelling wool to be used from birth to beyond death (woollen shrouds were compulsory). All that is left now are the buildings and, in the Weaver's Cottage, now a shop, Arthur Caton, the last of the local weavers, a big, bearded man who will sell you quality homespuns.

Go there, stay a few days – I can recommend 'The Swan', which contains real beer and good cooking. The other inn is 'The Bull', but I don't know it. YOU WILL BE BORED STIFF. For as with all English villages, and most towns, there is absolutely nothing to do, unless you do it yourself. Few walks – no leafy lanes, land is too valuable and is all cultivated. Now, even the hedges have gone for profit. No cinema, three or four pubs, Bingo occasionally. The church is the centre of life here, and Thaxted's present fame springs from this.

The presentation of the living lay, 70 years ago, with the Socialist Lady Warwick and in 1910 it was given to Conrad Noel, who was a most turbulent priest. He practised Christianity (the food eaten in his servants' kitchen was the same as that eaten in the family dining-room – an occurrence that is the exception even today); he abandoned the Official Prayer Book in favour of the English Medieval Rites. He did more, he set up a blood-red banner in the church (later, bearing the legend 'He hath made of one blood all Nations'). This was interpreted as the Communist flag, so Nazis from Cambridge and London came regularly to smash the place.

All these things led to a frightful row with the Bishop, and Thaxted was for a time put under an interdict – this means that no one is allowed to be born or marry or die in the parish. Noel, backed by the Churchwardens and most of the parish, won, but only eventually, and the next Bishop acknowledged his greatness, at his funeral.

One of Noel's many friends was Gustav Holst who came to organise the music in the church, and came to live in the town. Holst was the Head of Music at Morley College; so, if you are lucky you might go into the church one sunny summer afternoon and hear the Morley Singers giving their annual pilgrimage concert at the home of their Founder.

Noel died in 1942 and was succeeded by his son-in-law Jack Putterill, not so turbulent, but just as principled – he caused Lidice to be rebuilt after its destruction by the Nazis.

I first met Jack over 20 years ago, during a course at Clarence House (one of the Queen Anne houses, now belonging to the Essex Education people), at midsummer. I had spent the morning sitting in the town square – the Bull Ring – dressed in drag: skirt, shawl and bonnet, and with a very new three-month beard – surrounded by dancers, and knitting to entertain the crowds. In the afternoon was the Vicarage Fête with dancing on the lawn – all sorts, Morris, Country and Czech.

I never knew Jack well, although we sat on the same committee for some years, but I shall always remember the little priest in cassock and biretta (Anglican, remember); he retired two or three years ago. Personal reminiscences, 'red' priests – what has this to do with current customs? Ah! Well!

You might, perhaps, find yourself driving from London just after dark one Saturday evening in early summer. Coming round the corner into the High Street and down towards the Moot Hall. What's this? The whole square is jammed tight with people. The police won't be of much use tonight. Nothing for it but to abandon the car, well out of the way, and see what is going on. Hundreds of people, dozens of men in funny trousers and hats, ribbons and bells round their ankles, all gathered round an open space down by the Hall. A hush, and then a most peculiar tune is heard on a solo fiddle as down the hill from the church comes a file of men in red and white, led, until he retired, by Jack, the Vicar, all carrying reindeer horns. It's the Thaxted Morris Men dancing the oldest dance in the world: the Abbots Bromley Horn Dance, to its old haunting and strangely magical tune, their traditional item for this particular weekend. The file comes down before the Hall, turns into two lines, meet, retire, cross, round, hey and all over again; insistent, haunting, mysterious hunting magic. A survival from prehistory to ensure food for the dark of late winter. Brought here from Abbots Bromley in Staffordshire, by the Folk Revival. For that is just what it is, revival. This whole affair is the Thaxted Morris Ring Meeting, which dates from 1934.

Tomorrow shall be my dancing day,
I would my true Love did so chance
To see the legend of my play,
To call my true Love to the Dance.
Sing Oh, my Love, Oh, my Love, my Love, my Love,
This have I done for my true Love.

In 1910, Blanche Payling from Mary Neale's London Esperance Club came to teach country song and dance at the new Vicar's wife's request. (Miss Neale was a collaborator of Cecil Sharp and apparently the first actually to get people to *do* the dances they had collected. It was a tragedy that they later differed bitterly and publicly, seemingly over trivialities.) Folk music was an immediate success – after all, it wasn't very long since Thaxted's own traditional Morris had died out, also much indigenous song has been found.

Every year there is a Morris Ring meeting at Thaxted; for it was here in 1934 that the idea of the Ring as a federation of Morris Clubs was mooted and the Squire of the Thaxted Men, the late Alec Hunter, became the first Squire of the Ring. (Some of Alec's paintings are in the Victoria and Albert Museum – he was president of the Industrial Artists' Association.) The original six clubs have swollen to over a hundred. You won't go far now in England during the summer without finding one or other Morris side earning its beer money by dancing for you – making sunshine, rain, fertility or just plain amusement. But apart from the originating villages, Thaxted is their spiritual home and the annual meeting is probably more popular than the others held all over the country.

What exactly are these Ring Meetings? A Federation of

Clubs or single village sides is fair enough, but . . .? Well, they are exactly that – meetings of the clubs in the Federation to dance together for fellowship and goodwill and for the general benefit. All follow the same pattern; everybody gathers together at some central point on the Friday evening for a party and private dance, to lubricate and warm up for the main activities of the following day. On Saturday

Morris Men and Hobby Horse stride past the Moot Hall at Thaxted. (*Will Green*)

morning, all pile into cars and minibuses, driven by non-alcoholic wives and girl-friends, and go off in groups on planned routes to the surrounding country villages.

At around opening time everybody starts dancing. Gradually the groups of dancers work through the villages, nearer and nearer the centre, leaving trails of dry pubs behind them. In late afternoon they arrive for massed dancing in the Town Square. An hour of this and a short rest, and the women are abandoned! They apparently disappear to their own private hiding places! The men congregate in a handy hall for a feast. Now, this isn't a secret society any more than a Regimental Mess is, but it is private and I don't propose to talk of what goes on, beyond saying that it is a formal dinner with some speeches and a good deal of singing – I might say here that the average Morris Man is probably a better folk singer than the average folk singer.

The men emerge comfortable and happy, gather the

A Morris Side and their Hobby Horse dance outside a pub during the Thaxted Ring Meeting. (*British Tourist Authority*)

women from wherever they have secreted themselves, find their kit and drift down to the square for the evening's entertainment. Always at dusk, the Thaxted Men, as hosts, do the Horn Dance. All the other clubs do their turns interspersed with massed dances. The official evening ends with the massed dancers in 'Bonny Green Garters', the whole lot winding in file round the square and disappearing:

First for her stockings and then for her shoes,
And then for her bonny green garters.
A pair for me and a pair for you,
And a pair for they that comes after.

Unofficially afterwards, many, if not all, tend to gather at the pubs and dance and sing and soak and sweat until as long after closing time as possible.

Passing over the night, which is probably fertile, Sunday morning gives us a special Church Service at which all the Club Squires present their staffs of office at the altar, and maybe a side will dance, like 'David before the Lord', or more appropriately as Christ danced with the apostles in a ring at the Last Supper (*vide* Apocryphal Acts of St John). Afterwards, more dancing in the Bull Ring. Possibly there is a country dance in the afternoon – to keep the women happy – then home, tired but contented.

This is the Ring weekend meeting; the spectacular affair when you might find one or two hundred men dancing; every year at Thaxted, but several weekends at other places, changing each year.

Then there are the Thaxted Men's own days for dancing, particularly Whitsun, when only they dance, with no more than perhaps a few friends from outside. They will also dance for all important occasions as required – fêtes, concerts, etc.

But at all these you will be required, nay compelled, to buy your season's good luck, preferably several times over. The more you give, the more good luck you will have. No excuses are accepted. I went to see my own Club dance once; not having been to practice myself for some time, I had to pay – 'You'll get it back at your next practice,' I was told!

You need not worry too much about what the Morris is for. The men may tell tall stories about the obscene meaning of their gestures, they may tell of fertility, but for the purposes of Thaxted, and everywhere else we dance now, it is purely to enjoy ourselves and entertain you while we do it (well, perhaps not purely – it is after all a fertility rite!). 'We have made the people laugh, therefore there will be rain,' said the witch doctor.

There is dancing in London, massed dancing at that, but the essential magic is slightly lacking in Trafalgar Square, or by an Underground station entrance. Thaxted is the most predictable of the occasions for massed dancing, and the little town gives just the needed atmosphere, as do the Essex villages through which we dance on the Saturday morning tours. Elsewhere we may write of origins and rituals and the remaining traditions, but Thaxted has a magic in itself, which is enhanced by the dancing. Or am I prejudiced?

Go and see for yourself – it is the weekend after next. If not this time, then don't delay your visit too long, for the church spire is leaning slightly and is in the direct flight path from Stansted Airport. So, when (not if, for it is being done by stealth) Stansted officially becomes London's third air terminal and the big stuff comes in, the spire will fall.

I did go to Thaxted that year, on the Saturday, and with Brian's expert guidance found myself driving across hilly farmland with open fields, at this summer time filled with waving wheat. Then suddenly, coming over the brow of a hill was the delicate spire of a church, rising up, unexpectedly like Salisbury's slender steeple. Reaching up towards a cloud-shadowed sky from a backcloth of undulating roof-tops, it seems to spring up as though aiming towards heaven, a slim, tapering finger which beckons both men and God to a meeting. There are many fine old houses as well as the Moot Hall. The church is a real delight. Inside it is open and spacious and filled with light. The copies of the Abbots Bromley horns rest close to the font and within the bright space of the nave – ideal for the dances which take place on church festivals. The pagan rites are welcomed in this House of God. The church's fine bells are also dedicated to the Dance.

The village streets seem strangely deserted this lunch-time, although we know there must be hundreds of Morris Men and their friends in the area. Clutching cameras and tape-recorders

Inside Thaxted church, a space of light and air ideal for dancing, music and prayer. (*Edwin Smith*)

we set off to explore. 'Try "The Bull" first, they ought to be there,' says the expert – and then, wandering down an otherwise deserted street, beer-pots in hands, are two Morris Men. Londoners, by the look of it, for they are wearing the startling livery of yellow and black of the Westminster Men. Following them down the street we came upon a pyramid of Morris Men, involved in some custom which, though it may not be dancing, may well have something to do with fertility, for they are scrambling in through the upstairs window of a cottage opposite a pub. Judging by giggling girls' voices, they are not alone! After a while they emerge downstairs to plunge into the throng which is packing the yard and 'The Bull' inn.

After a battle to the bar for a noggin and a sandwich we feel ready to face some of the dancing which is getting underway outside. There are lots of Morris Men, mostly clutching mugs of ale, or musical instruments, and in the centre of the yard, leaving a space barely large enough for six or eight lusty lads to move, the dance is going on. 'Jocky to the Fair', 'Bells of London', 'Beansetting', 'The Cuckoo's Nest', and all the weird and wonderful tunes of the Morris, wherever it is found. Some dancers use hefty sticks and clout each other's poles in the dance; some more delicate manoeuvres are carried out with handkerchiefs. Sometimes the accompaniment is pipe and tabor, or accordion, or fiddle, or the whole lot. Sides of men from London, Essex and Surrey dance; a team of North Country Sword Dancers make their way to the stage and dance the slow, intricate paces of the Longsword.

This is one of the oldest dances, probably dating to a time when men commonly carried swords, and this version uses blunt weapons with a handle at each end, or sometimes a bunch of ribbons instead of a point. The six dancers are joined together by their swords and begin the stately steps of this dance. To the steady throb of the music, and the clumping of their wooden-soled clogs, they move round and round, under arches of swords, over blades held near the ground, always keeping firm grasp of their swords which are woven among them as they form a tight ring. Suddenly, with a clash and a wrench the blades are fixed into the lock, the symbol familiar as the badge of the English Folk Dance and Song Society, and the leader holds up the six-pointed star. In some versions of this dance one of the team places his head inside the lock and it is broken around him, as if he is the sacrificial victim, which rite it probably echoes from the

A Morris Man holds aloft the locked swords at the end of the Longsword Dance at Thaxted in Essex.

remote past. Again the dancer is 'revived', copying the sun that returns after midwinter, the green life that burgeons forth each spring – the whole point of these old customs.

These are the men's sacred dances, which ensured fertility and

luck. The white clothes are worn in honour of that most ancient deity, the White Goddess, she who was the first Mother of Creation, and of whom the Virgin Mary is but the latest in a long line of successors. The ribbons are uniforms to each side, chosen colours and symbols which relate to their home town or village. The Portsmouth Men wear sailors' hats and dance a kind of hornpipe to the tune 'Portsmouth', made popular by Mike Oldfield. The old side from Bampton in Oxfordshire wear cricket caps, and some sides have taken to bowler hats, or more often straw hats with flowers and badges of places visited. The pads of bells strapped below the knees, and the bright streamers are all designed to drive away harm and evil influences from crops and cattle, from hearth and barn. The leaping and gesturing enacts the way corn should grow, or the manner of tilling the soil or harvesting the crops. Many of the dances were spring ones, but are now seen pretty well all the year round.

Each Morris side will have six or eight men for each dance, and often they have a Fool who is certainly the best dancer among them. 'Six fools and one dancer,' goes one saying. Occasionally there is a hermaphrodite figure, called a Betty in the south, where a Morris man gets up in drag. Many sides have a Hobby Horse which may have the head of a horse, although there are some fascinating variations. The Westminster Men have a fine Unicorn; there are stags, bulls, goats, and, of course, dragons. These represent the life-force, the virile, fertilising stallion and so on, and as well as dancing through the middle of the hey or set, they take part in the Folk Plays which, with the Sword Dance, make up the trilogy of festival traditions of the common folk.

As well as the musicians, who may be playing pipes, fiddles, accordions or drums, there will be a Squire who organises the dancing, calls for some sets, and a Bagman who looks after the sticks, instruments and other odds and ends which have to be lugged about to outdoor locations. Morris is very much tied up with pubs – most of the summer dances are found outside real ale hostelries. (When there is a tour including pubs with the wrong beer, supplies of a more suitable fluid are laid in.)

As well as Thaxted with its 3 days of Morris, there are several Ring Meetings elsewhere, in West Country villages and even in central London. I once got mixed up with one in Taunton, which

The Fool with his traditional inflated pig's bladder dances with the Bampton Men.

was an incredible experience. During a visit to Glastonbury I happened to hear the tinkle of Morris bells which drew me like an addict to his drug, and discovered a side dancing outside St John's in the High Street. They explained they were part of a Ring which would dance next day in Taunton. On the Sunday we found a whole bevy of Hobby Horses, Stags, Dragons (there are several splendid ones in the West Country), and flower-decked Squires' staffs forming an archway under which hordes of Morris Men passed as they came out of the church after a service of blessing. (Whether the Morris blessed the church or vice versa, I don't know.) Anyway, as the pubs opened they got down to some serious dancing in the High Street, which had been closed to traffic on their behalf.

Seeking refreshment we shoved our way into a posh-looking hotel nearby which was already stuffed with Morris Men, players and their molls. Soon we were fortified with glasses of slightly

The traditional fiddler, accordion player and drummer add music to the tinkle of bells and stamp of feet at the Morris Festival.

sparkling golden elixir of life, brewed or fermented locally, and sought somewhere to rest weary feet. In the lounge we managed to perch on the edge of a table in this haven of relative peace. After a few moments one of the musicians, resting there, laid his fiddle across his knee and began quietly to play one of the Fool's Jigs. Someone else produced some spoons, and Brian, a Morris dancer at heart, pulled two sparkling white handkerchiefs from his pockets and, walking-boots notwithstanding, started to dance on about one square foot of floor. 'You're a Morris man, then,' someone said, and they began to sing. Most of the tunes they dance to have words, with varying degrees of rudeness, but these aren't often heard. It is certainly an experience to be in a bar full of slightly inebriated (on atmosphere as much as beer) Morris Men, who are determined to sing and play and dance their magic. They didn't throw us out either, though the walls were shaking a bit before closing time.

There are a number of Morris Ring meetings and festivals all over this country, so look out for the announcements. Morris is a growing interest – last year at Thaxted there was a side of American Morris Men, dressed in red! It is just beginning to catch on over there, and though its origins are lost in the mists of time, the number of sides, and the young and older chaps taking up this activity which combines exercise, music, friendly companionship and beer so well, is growing all the time. More power to their elbows, and knees, say I!

CHAPTER 5

Modern rites at a Stone Age timepiece

> Awake, for morning in the bowl of night Has cast the stone
> that puts the stars to flight,
> And lo, the Hunter of the East has caught a 'sarsen boulder'
> in a net of Light.
>
> Apologies to Omar Khayyám

Most people probably think that the Druids were quelled by Julius Caesar, and hardly expect to come across any in full regalia in Wessex, but come midsummer, folk could be in for a surprise.

Stonehenge, that mysterious ancient construction of sarsen stones, linked together for aeons like a circle of Greek dancers, alone in the middle of a desolate and uninhabited plain, is the setting for the modern Druids' solstice ceremonies. Like many of the other festivals, the exact date of the midsummer solstice, when the sun moves out of Gemini into Cancer, may alter slightly from year to year, but it is generally the 22 or 23 June, and this is the occasion of three ceremonies held before the assembled masses, as such rites must have been in times long ago. However, there are a lot of snags today, for the monument comes under the jurisdiction of the Department of the Environment and is protected by it from vandals, tourists and, at midsummer, the Druids and their followers, by miles of barbed wire, spotlights, and large Alsatian dogs. Despite all this, the ceremonies are permitted and can be extremely fascinating.

As far as we are concerned the moment of midsummer is when the sun is at its highest point, for then it changes into its downward arc, to reach its lowest point about 22 December. These moments of solar time have been recognised for thousands of years, and many of the rings of standing stones put up by our ancestors are concerned with marking the positions of sun and moon and some of the stars. Only in the last few decades when

The Swordbearer leads the Druids to their positions before midsummer dawn. (*Will Green*)

computer technology has been employed in investigating the Stone Age methods which caused these stones to be shaped, carried and erected in accurate positions, have we been able to discover the skill with which they were placed.

The sun, rising at midsummer, is to be seen on a clear day emerging from the shadow of the Hele Stone, and setting close against the remaining column of the great trilithon. The spring

Overleaf Midsummer's Day dawns over the vast, massive sarsen stones, looming out of the landscape at Stonehenge, protected now from visitors' touch.

and autumnal equinoctial setting suns fall into the gaps in the other two huge trilithons like pennies going into the maws of slot machines.

What happens then to celebrate this high point of the solar year, which must have been important for at least 4,000 years? Now there are three rituals, the first of which takes place at midnight before the solstice. A party of London-based Druids arrives by coach, and its members prepare themselves for a long vigil of ceremony and procession which will occupy their next 12 hours. The first part of the celebration involves a longish walk in the dark to a round barrow about half a mile from Stonehenge. Dressed in their white robes and head-dresses, carrying tall banners with symbolic designs, a band of Druids, led by the herald, sets off into the dark. The ghostly column winds along the rough track, stumbling over the rutted chalk under a gibbous moon among fleeting clouds. It is very dark but the orange glow of the lights of distant Salisbury illumines one section of the sky; the rest is touched only with a brush of stars, glittering in darkness. It is very quiet, except for careful footsteps and the wind soughing through tall grass. On this great plain the wind is seldom still, and it whispers its age-old secrets most often to an uninhabited land and empty sky.

Onward through the darkness, here and there interrupted by flashes of torches and quiet conversation from the followers, most of the Druids keep silence and plod forward in contemplation. It is their big night and they seem filled with the atmosphere of it. Out here in the night the plain seems endless, untouched by man and open only to the Creative God who made it, blessed it, and seems to have deserted it. Among this shuffling throng one feels very lonely and somewhat awed and diminished by the vast darkness, so different from night in the city.

Comparatively few of the huge crowd which normally gathers for the midsummer ceremonies are taking part in this first dark march; most who make this mysterious journey have come from London in the coach or know what is to happen. Others, in the great car park near the monument, have noticed the white robes and banners and followed out of curiosity. The procession winds up and down hills and finally emerges into a field of tall grass, or perhaps it is standing corn. In the centre there rises the curve of a barrow, like the breast of the Earth Mother, green and comely against a black sky.

At last the party gathers together in this hour of dark vigil, seemingly alone in a night where the sky is enormous, and if the clouds have drifted away, white with the myriads of stars of the Milky Way. Watch, you may see a shooting star arching across the blackness, or be able to discern some of the many man-made satellites which roam the heavens, like planets winging their curved journey overhead. All is still; the white robes, here and there picked out with torchlight, resemble strange, ghostly figures from some distant past, waiting for the purpose to be revealed. One of the Triad speaks, to tell of those people long gone, on whose grave the night watchers have gathered; those who watched the sky by day and night and planned the placing of those marking stones, which dawn will show. Who were those antique scientists who built and raised the markers on the horizon that still, 4,000 years or so later, show up and indicate the position of the rising sun that is to come, the setting of the moon and other significant phases in the year-long dance of solar life?

Perhaps there is a sermon, an indication of how we, the inheritors, should manage our land, our planet, the knowledge bequeathed by those who came before and raised this mound so long ago. We do not know their race or their names, we do not know why they needed to set up stones to show the position of the sun at solstice and equinox, yet their handiwork has endured the passage of time and we remember them for their wisdom. Perhaps their long forgotten sciences will be recalled and their motivation understood before the twenty-first century – who knows? We are but travellers on this planet Earth, who come and go and perhaps return in some future age, but on the eve of the summer solstice we are silent witnesses to the memory of those who came before, both recently and many years or centuries ago. Now is the time of recollection and in this spoken vigil, in darkness and far from the city's glare, we stand before nature and come to know how small we are, under an endless sky, upon a limitless plain, which could be limbo for all that we can tell.

From a dark fringe of clouds upon the distant horizon the moon lifts upwards, curving slowly, white and shimmering with mist or threat of rain to come. Even midsummer is not guaranteed to be dry in this land of verdant pastures and drizzly afternoons. In the darkness the scent of the grass is heady, and where some distant field has been mown for a second crop of hay, it wafts upon the ever present wind, reminding the town-dwellers of lost childhoods among green fields, of freshly-cut lawns and cricket on the village green. The rite continues, hands are linked in friendship, and perhaps in grateful acknowledgement that we are not alone in this strange, open place; a ragged circle of shadows in darkness on a black field, pause and wonder for that moment of harmony.

The words are spoken, perhaps a prayer or invocation to the Great Mother or the Bright Lord; the speech is whisked into the night, unheard and unremembered. The circle breaks and staggers back into line. Torches are found and flash their puny beams upon the white, chalky track; pale Druid forms lead the wanderers back from the wilderness, from some strange experience unlikely in an electric-lit city where seldom are the streets still. Overhead the stars glitter like frozen fireworks, silver and pale colours. Something has been lost and something gained in this strange vigil, and those who come back towards the road, where cars lance the night with their twin swords of light, are not quite the same as those who set out on the first journey of discovery.

Gradually the real world impinges upon the senses. Traffic hums along the road, much of it directed into the car parks in this darkest time before dawn. Vans and campers crowd the tarmac space, and sellers of hot drinks and pies ply their nocturnal wares, most welcome in the cooling wind. Druids wend their way to their coach to prepare for the next part of the ceremony, that of greeting the dawn, a couple of hours away. Here and there soft notes of strummed guitars vie with late-night radio programmes. Blanketed forms huddle uncomfortably in small cars, or slumber unregarded on grass verges. Those who are prepared for this occasion are cocooned warmly in quilted sleeping bags, or under the shelter of tiny tents, blue or orange or less noticeable green. The elite of nocturnal rites have camping vans, brew up on their own gas stoves, and sleep warm and cosy on let-down beds, lulled by soft stereo, curtained from the dark and as well protected from the elements as they would be in their own homes.

Around the mighty, ancient stones searchlights sweep the air, casting unnatural shadows of barbed wire upon the sleeping grass. Grey dog-forms patrol, watching lest any reveller in the hours before dawn should seek to find a good vantage point, or write some slogan on the stones. In times gone by – well, a decade or so – the whole place would be athrong with folk, singing, crowding the spaces between the stones, wandering on the grass, playing instruments and getting ready for a great festival.

Now the army has the situation under its control with wire and patrols and orders through walkie-talkies.

Night passes, and cars, vans, buses and motor cycles flood in from all over the place. The nearest village, Amesbury, is about 3 miles away, the nearest railway station, goodness knows how far. Pilgrims have hitch-hiked and travelled many miles to be at Stonehenge before midsummer sunrise. They come in all shapes and sizes, from England and from distant lands, all waiting to see, if the weather is kind, a confirmation of Stone Age technology, the accuracy of the placement of the marking arch which frames the rising sun. Although it is not easy to get within the wire entanglements unless you are actually taking part in the sunrise rituals, it does not stop huge crowds coming, simply to be there, as if it were an obligation to make the pilgrimage this midsummer day.

Folk come in jeans and jumpers, in fancy dress, in city suits, Druid robes, and perhaps evening dress, having come on after some other midsummer party. Some shiver in sunshine clothes, others huddle in blankets or thick cloaks, well wrapped against the pre-dawn chill. There is always a stir about the Druids' coach where enquirers flock to ask for information, to discover how they can actually get in on the dawn ceremony, to ask those heaps of questions about what it is all for; why it is being continued; how did the Druids build Stonehenge; and so on. These are patiently answered, explanations given, and in the still dark night the participants get ready for the next ceremony. White robes are donned, over layers of woollies if they are wise, for sunrise or not, it is extremely cold when you are standing about in the middle of Salisbury Plain.

Long before there is any light in the sky, the Druids' herald emerges, followed by four volunteer Dionarchs who will guard the sacred elements on the marker stones as light grows and the sky pales. A small party sets out on the hazardous journey under the road and out among the towering stones. They have another lonely wait, each one abandoned at one of the outermost points of this great monument, to stand watching over the mystical symbols until the pre-sunrise party comes to gather all into the centre of the circle for the ceremony. Among the wire and trailing lighting cables it is a weird walk, almost a cross between ancient rite and science fiction set. Brilliant arc lights flare and throw dark, mysterious shadows of stones and Druids to confuse and dazzle the eyes. Alone, the four element bearers are left as the

herald returns to the car park to collect the main party. In the east the sky begins to lighten, and stars in the quarter start to fade. The westering moon falls into cloud wrack, and soon dark, silhouetted trees will engulf her light, leaving only points of starfire in midheaven, and billows of windblown cloud scudding across the dark.

In the car park the Druid celebrants emerge, dressed in long white robes and head-dresses, the officers wearing pendants with symbolic designs. The Chief Druid carries a shepherd's crook wreathed with oak leaves, and is escorted by his own banner-bearers and attendants as he progresses through the processional to gather in the sacred elements. These are represented by some bread or holy biscuits, and salt, for the earth, a silver cup for water, an incense burner whose sweet scent represents fire, and a single red rose for air. These have been placed and watched over since the first part of the ceremony.

Although there is still some time before the sun rises the sky is growing lighter, and darker clouds sidle across the paling sky like a vast flock of grey sheep swept forward by the impelling wind, which seldom rests from harrying the grasses and sparse trees on Salisbury Plain. The floodlights seem dimmer, the horizon sharper, a black rim to the world. Watchers scan the sky for gaps of blue, in the hope they will join to give a clear sky, at least along the eastern rim. The pale-robed Druids throng together and draw out like wool upon a skilled spinner's distaff, forming into an uneven procession to begin the assault course leading to their ritual positions within the great, looming stones. Banners waver and lunge against the morning breeze, each with three attendants to keep it in check; white, nun-like head-dresses flutter as the long column, led by the herald and sword-bearer, moves onwards, towards the waiting dawn.

The crowds hum and mutter with anticipation, peering at the white-robed figures, staring at the lightening sky, jostling to see against the dark stone silhouettes whether the sun will rise in its appointed place. Catcalls and music echo around the huge throng. There are probably far more pilgrims who are drawn to this festival than any other, attracted to be at a pile of great boulders, set into formal patterns by the hand of man lost aeons ago, for a purpose which even modern computer technology is at

Dr Thomas Maughan, the late Chief Druid with the bunch of symbolic oak leaves awaits the sunrise at Stonehenge. (*Will Green*)

a loss to explain. They are not paid to be there, they are not forced to attend by State or Church; it is not easy to get to the place, nor is it normal to be up and about at 3 a.m. in order to watch a small number of dressed-up individuals with no recognised faith perform a ceremony to mark the sunrise of midsummer. They have all come of their own free will, to be there in case the sun shows clearly, and in case some strange revelation should occur. They are the latest pilgrims to honour the One Light by their presence, drawn by some inner impulsion which defies logical explanation, yet they are there, ready and waiting to greet the dawn in their own way.

The procession halts near the southernmost marker mound outside the great ellipse of sarsens, and asks enlightenment with the prayer led by the Chief Druid: 'Let us contemplate the super-essential Light of lights, the unconquerable Sun of suns, the unquenched Flame within each one.' The ritual salutation of the rising sun has begun, as it always has, somewhere. The procession winds onwards, seeking a way between the wire and lamps, put there to protect the monument which stands as a mighty cathedral open to the sky, where worship of the Creative Force, the Life-giving Light, has been performed for thousands of years. Not always here among these towering grey stones, can rites take place, for Church and State have frowned upon such public practices. But the ceremony has not been forgotten, though it may have been overlooked. Today these modern Druids are permitted to worship and hold festivals in this strange and sacred place, more often haunt of tourists than of priests.

'We are gathered within this place of Light and have left outside all disturbing thoughts . . .' the congregation continues. 'Universal Majesty, Verity and Love Infinite, all reverence to the Holy, the Pure, the Liberating Doctrine, all reverence to the Brotherhood of the Elect, and to all that is noblest and best in Mankind.' The Chief continues onward to collect the symbols until all are brought together and led towards the grove of sarsen pillars. One of the companions asks: 'Why are we gathered in to this sacred meeting?' – and is answered from the Triad of Officers: 'To do reverence to the Word that was made known to our forebears, and to acknowledge our debt to those who preserved the Truth. . . .'

The Chief Druid, standing beneath his banner, watches for the rising sun to lift over the Hele Stone.

Cairdeachas

The mystical elements are brought forward and placed upon what is sometimes called the 'Slaughter Stone' which lies near the Hele Stone towards the east. It is a fallen pillar which marked the end of the processional way from another sacred site. The Druids form lines beside this recumbent stone and then, following their officers, go up to the Hele Stone to swear a renewal of the covenant between Heaven and Earth. Hele is an old word for 'hold to', and some modern oaths include the word in the phrase 'Hele, conceal and never reveal . . .' – so it seems appropriate that such a bond should be made upon this great sarsen, which stands between the rising sun and the centre of the Henge. Water is also blessed in the name of the Great Mother so that the link between Earth and Mankind may also be renewed and strengthened. Finally the file of white-robed sun priests enters the tall arches of great stones, rough-carved perhaps 5,000 years ago, fretted and worn by wind and sun, yet unbowed by time. Within the ring of their shadows the holy elements are laid out upon a linen cloth at the centre of the circle. Branches of oak, long associated with the Druid cult, are placed symbolically upon the fire.

Tension is rising now for it is only a few minutes to the moment of dawn. Watchers outside the circle crane their necks and peer towards the eastern horizon. From inside the standing stones the words of the ritual are silenced, and the Herald's trumpet rings out, accompanied by cheers and shouts from those outside the wire. Slightly to the north of east, when the sky is clear and the horizon unveiled of mist, the great golden orb of the sun edges up to glow over the peak of the Hele Stone which stands out black against an orange sky. There is a hush, a whisper of indrawn breath and a great sigh before the cheers break out. The sun has risen in his appointed place and rolls upward, blazing into an azure sky. Pink clouds blush rose and yellow and pale to glimmer in the rising light. Greys become green of grass and distant trees, mist pearls and vanishes. 'Arise, O Sun, let the darkness of night fade in thy glorious light. . . .'

There is a salutation to Nature, to the wisdom of the past, the skills which caused the sun's motion to be watched and understood, his path marked with pillars of hewn stone, his downsetting recorded and tall trilithons raised wherein his motion could be caught and exact moments of time known. When these heavy stones were first put up, the rising sun stood one diameter higher, and instead of shyly peeping over the Hele

Stone, stood upon it, a glowing golden ball, framed in the arch of linked sarsens. What patience caused these hard rocks to be shaped and hauled upright by men who did not have the use of metal, and worked each one with other stones, pounding and rubbing, to square and smooth the correct shape? How were they raised up and held until each matching capstone with its deep indentations was fitted on to carven pegs at the top of each pillar? These forerunners of the press-stud met with such accuracy and strength that many are still standing as they were first made to stand so long ago. Each linking stone is shaped to deceive the eye, so that it appears square, looking upwards, yet it actually tapers; each is slightly curved to fit the ellipse in which these mighty boulders stand. No mean feat for Stone Age men! Did they raise up the pillars with logs and construct platforms of trees to lift each stone slowly into place? Or did they sing, as legend has it, at some mighty festival, and cause the Hanging Stones to rise into position? Or did the first Merlin lift them by magic, as Geoffrey of Monmouth tells us in his Histories of the Kings of Britain, having brought them from the Mountains of Killarus in Ireland? Were they put up by spacemen as a marker for their landing place, or did our ancestors slide them into place up ramps of snow, some bitter winter when the herds and flocks were safe in byre and pen, and barren fields were hard beyond the working of wooden ploughshare or spade? Who knows?

Within the space of light and shadow this summer dawn, these questions may rise as concentration falters from lack of sleep. The ceremony continues with sprinklings of blessed water, with the scent of sweet incense wafted around the ring of watching Druids; prayers are intoned, but it is now morning and the air feels different. The promise has been fulfilled, between sun and man; the ancient builders' plan has been proved, the vigil has been kept and the covenants renewed. Above the scent of incense distant whiffs of coffee brewing up drift temptingly towards the onlookers at the rite. The Druids gather up their mystic objects, re-form the procession and with a final prayer for peace, intoned by one of the Officers, the white-clad column sets off across the dewy grass in the early morning light, in quest of less metaphysical things, like a bit of rest and breakfast. By now it feels like the afternoon to those who have kept vigil since the first ceremony, but it is scarcely 5 a.m.

The celebrations of the Druids are not yet finished, for there is still the midday service to perform, when members of the public are allowed into the monument and can participate in a traditional symbolic feast of bread and wine. Of course, by now it is accepted that the original Druids had nothing to do with the building of Stonehenge and other, similar monuments, for they were the priests and priestesses of the Celtic people who lived in Britain about 700 B.C., and whose influence was finally quelled in Anglesey by the Romans under Suetonius Paulinus in A.D. 61. The great sarsen blocks were shaped and lifted into place over quite a few hundreds of years, probably around 2,000 years B.C. Carbon dating methods on deer antler picks discovered under some of the stones, and on cremated human bones found in pits close to the circular ditch, have gradually pushed the date of this great monument of Stone Age skill further and further back. It is now thought to pre-date the Pyramids and other ancient structures, of which some historians had considered these mighty, linked stones to be a poor copy.

Although we now see only a few of the arching capstones in place, the original Henge consisted of a complete ring of joined uprights, inside which there were five great trilithons, each a gateway of three enormous stones, forming apertures through which the setting sun could be watched from a central place. There are also blue stones, smaller and bluish-grey in colour, which form an ellipse inside the main ring. These are the foreign stones, brought in some manner either from the Prescelly Mountains in South Wales, or, as legend has it, from Ireland. This kind of rock, dolerite and rhyolite, is found in both locations. It is usually considered that the stones were carried on rafts along the coast and up the rivers, to be finally hauled on sledges up from the nearest stream to the site. Again, they could have been sledged on ice if the winters were cold enough.

Archaeological evidence has shown that there are many stages of the construction of the monument, and that its earlier forms differed considerably from what is now visible. The earliest stages included the great circular ditch and bank which can still be seen round most of the site, but from the very oldest construction, someone must have been watching the distant horizon and marking the rising and setting places of the sun and moon and various stars. Probably the first markers were wooden posts, and later, once the positions were certain, these would be replaced by stones of various sizes. According to evidence worked out by feeding into computers data on the positions of all the standing stones, and those that are missing or fallen, and the rising and setting points of the sun and moon and some of the major stars, it was found that every stone is important, some stones acting as markers in up to seven alignments. The five great trilithon arches which used to form the centre-piece of this neolithic monument, stand in a horse-shoe shape (often symbolic in itself, to keep away harm), and provide narrow slots into which both sun and moon appear. The midsummer sun may rise over the Hele Stone today as a flash, although allowing for the tilt of this large rock having increased, and the position of the rising sun in about 2,000 B.C. being slightly higher, a watcher at the time of Stonehenge's building would see the sun stand as a complete disc, perched on the Hele Stone. The downsetting midsummer sun falls between the uprights of the greatest trilithon, like a ball into a trap. The midwinter sunrise is observed through the right-hand end arch (facing towards the Hele Stone), and sets in the left-hand one; the other pair of arches marks the rising and setting points of the moon.

Outside the main area of standing stones are four fairly insignificant mounds, where the Druids abandon the Dionarchs before the dawn ceremony. These mounds, two of which still have standing stones, form an exact rectangle; had the Henge been built anywhere else, this figure would be far less accurate. Every part of this ancient, mysterious construction seems to have a specific reason. The stones which have never fallen mark precisely the rising and setting points of the luminaries, whereas the sarsens which have been replaced by the then Ministry of Works, in the 1950s, are not so exact; in some cases the error is about 10 inches out of true. Modern research is tracing marks made on the horizon which would have acted as foresights with the stone arches as backsights on this enormous surveying instrument. Watchers from a central position would have been able to plot the movements of many of the heavenly bodies, and it seems likely that there was a settlement of priests or scientists on permanent lookout.

One of the most mysterious aspects of this strange place is that there was probably a method of predicting eclipses. Around the perimeter of the site are fifty-six pits, named after their discoverer, John Aubrey. These Aubrey Holes are carefully dug and evenly spaced, and though there is evidence that several of them were used as tombs, this was probably not their original purpose. They would have shown up white against the green grass, and Dr Gerald Hawkins suggests they were a computer system used by the priests to keep track of the years. By placing six stones or other markers, of two different colours, 9, 9, 10, 9, 9, and 10 holes apart, and all moved one hole anticlockwise each year, a particular marker at a specific hole would indicate an eclipse of the sun or moon. By watching such heavenly events and correcting the system it would have been possible to predict that, should the midwinter full moon rise over the Hele Stone, there would be an eclipse. The eclipse cycle is regular, but not obviously so, as events occur in 18, 19, 19 years, rather too long for the average person to remember. The priesthood would have been able to inform the people of the dates of the seasons, warn them of possible severe weather, no doubt, and mysteriously foretell eclipses. A simple system with the fifty-six holes and only three markers would work just as well. Watchers would be aware that the moon at the time of an eclipse rises only a short while – about 15 minutes – before the sunset, and later in the night is eclipsed by the earth's shadow, so they could tell the people when to watch for the phenomenon.

It is likely that the exact 29½-day lunar cycle was also marked in some way, perhaps by moving a marker round the fifty-nine blue stone circle, twice a day. By watching sun and moon rises, plotting eclipses and lunar months, these ancient priests would have known the date exactly, within the solar year. They could fix the times of planting and harvesting, of putting the bulls and rams among the herds and flocks, or show the times of festivals to celebrate the longest day, or the longest night. Within this huge temple/computer of stones perhaps 4,000 years ago there were midsummer vigils and celebrations, and maybe the priests and priestesses would pray to the Sun and make offerings to his life-giving power. Perhaps there were huge gatherings of people at the solstices and equinoxes, at seed-time and harvest, and perhaps the greatest stones were seen to dance as implied by their old name – The Giants' Dance.

Is it not likely that among these ancient arches, and in other, less elaborate circles of standing stones still found on hillside and moorland from Cornwall to the Shetlands, in Wales and most of England where there are rocks to build them with, that watchers knew the time of year, and held festival then? It seems most probable that from such accurate observations of the interaction of sun and moon and earth, and some of the stars, special dates were set aside to celebrate, to dance and feast, and maybe make offerings. The Romans may have accused the Celtic priests of burning felons alive in wicker baskets, but the logistics of such a punishment are a bit improbable; after all, wickerwork would burn much faster than live human flesh. Did the ancient clergy burn effigies of basketwork, the forerunners of the Green Men who still appear at festivals and fêtes? These foliate masks are found on many old churches and cathedrals, no doubt carved there by masons who knew many ancient secrets, handed down with their stone-cutting craft. Indeed, it is from such masons that modern Druids derive their heritage.

As with any ancient, secret organisation, it is difficult after a gap of 2,000 years or so to know for certain what sort of things the original Druids did, for though they were extremely learned in all sorts of matters, their teaching and religious beliefs were never written down. There are many early accounts from Roman and Greek sources, but these tend to be towards the end of their priesthood, and may not be correct; also, the Romans in particular were very anti-Druid, and finally had the last of them slaughtered upon the Holy Mountain near Holyhead in Anglesey.

It is generally thought that there were three sorts of Druids; some were mainly concerned with history and genealogies, with poetry and verse-making, music and the recording of events; these were the Bards. There was also a number of initiates concerned with teaching, law and astronomy/astrology, and possibly mathematics; these were called Vates, or sometimes Ovates, which term is still used today by one of the modern Orders of Druids. Finally, the Druids proper were priests, concerned with religious belief and practice. According to some records they had a Trinity of Gods called Hesu or Jesu, Taranis, and Belinus, whose symbol was a tree, cut roughly in the form of a cross. They were also magicians and healers, skilled in what might be called natural healing, by laying on of hands, and the uses of herbs and plants. Even the title Druid is often thought to have derived from *drus*, the oak tree, with which they were traditionally associated. Mistletoe, Sir James Frazer's 'Golden Bough', is another plant long linked with Druids, who were supposed to cut it at midwinter, near enough our Christmas, with a golden sickle, and let it fall into a clean, white linen cloth. Some authorities have it that the sacred mistletoe was cut from an oak tree, although our mistletoe, *Viscum album*, seldom grows on oak but rather apple, sacred in its own right, or lime trees. This plant was known as 'All Heal', and even now is thought to contain healing chemicals which are difficult to analyse. Ovid refers to Druids singing and dancing beneath oak trees, so once again the sacred dance which still occurs at many festivals gets a mention.

Druids were diviners, and from them it is said that the adage 'Truth lies at the bottom of a well' derives, for by looking down into the water it was possible either to study the moon and stars reflected, or use it like a crystal ball for scrying, looking into the future. They seem always to have been associated with springs and wells, and also, each group of Druids had its sacred grove. The apprenticeship was long, so maybe the novice had to plant some trees to form his sanctuary, and by the time he had studied for 20 years to master all the Druidic law, he would have a well-grown wood for his use. This may sound a long training, but it is no longer than it takes for a doctor or vet or architect to qualify, if he begins school at about 5 years old, and gets his degree at the age of 25. Where the training of the old priests differs from today's studies is that the students then did not write things down, nor refer to books or manuscripts. They had to commit everything to memory, as have all people who cannot read or write. The human memory is capable of a great deal if it is pushed. Bards would remember and retell long stories and legends, the lists of forebears of the kings and nobles, and all the information which had been handed down to them.

There seem to have been public festivals, rather like the modern Gorseddau where poetry and prose and music are performed before an audience, when the Druid priests made the offerings of animals and flowers for the festival. Even today church fêtes and local medieval-type fairs have ox roasts, or ram or deer barbecues, and these are not considered especially barbaric. Because they were particularly associated with the Sun, not so much as a deity but as a symbol, for they worshipped the Son behind the Sun, the solstices in June and December and the equinoxes in March and September when day and night are of equal length, are usually regarded as their main feasts. These are still kept by the modern successors, of whom there are three Orders in London as well as Welsh, Cornish and Breton Bards. The Eisteddfodau are probably also survivals from this ancient tradition of public presentation of poetry and song, originally part of their worship.

The ancient Druids seem to have been great travellers, and turned up wherever there were men of learning. Abaris travelled to Greece and conversed with Strabo in fine, fluent Greek. He was dressed in a plaid, held in place with a gilded belt, and long trousers – not the white robes that one might expect – but Druids were allowed to wear six colours; only the kings wore seven different ones. (See the Royal Stuart tartan.) The Celts of Britain were traders in tin, hides, hunting dogs, lead, and woollen cloth, and their sea and land routes covered most of the then known world. Wherever the merchants went, the Druids went too, partly as priests, partly as navigators from their knowledge of the stars, and partly as doctors or teachers to spread knowledge or gain it where they could. The British Druids were considered the most learned, and students from Gaul came to be taught here in the great universities.

Although the Romans obliterated the priestly functions of the Druids, their followers took to the Christian Jesus quite early, seeing Him as a version of Hesu, the Branch (as the Messiah was known in Hebrew), part of their own sacred tree symbol, which also tied up with the Crucifixion. Probably the actual teachings and healing and other forms of secret knowledge continued to be taught, and some of the traditional dates for feasts and celebrations carried on until they, too, were merged with the festivals of the Christian Church. The early monks seem to have continued rather in the manner of the Druids, and some of the differences of opinion between the Church of Rome and the Celtic Church were differences between the Druidic and Christian traditions. Druids were married and their sons inherited their positions; this also applied to the Celtic Church. The Celtic tonsure consisted of shaving the forehead rather than a patch on top of the head; these and other similar practices caused difficulties between the branches of the early Church.

Although in the Welsh and Irish Bardic traditions the notion of the Druid priest-magician continued, recurring in various legends and tales, the organised groves of Druids and Druidesses had been wiped out by the Romans. Certainly their knowledge of astrology, healing and divination continued, being used by the ordinary folk, and the dates of the festivals, which had now been absorbed into the Christian calendar, were still being celebrated in the old way. Possibly some of this ancient knowledge has been preserved in fragments even up to the present day. Merlin, King Arthur's magician tutor is sometimes thought of as a Druid, for he had many of their traditional skills of fortune-telling and healing, according to the stories.

There is no evidence that the Druids were directly associated with Stonehenge, certainly in its oldest form, for the people who were its designers were the pre-Celtic folk, archaeologists tell us. However, if the Druid priests were wise in such things as astronomy and fixing the dates of the calendars, and if they were associated with worship in which the Sun was an important symbol, is it not likely that they would have known about this great solar sanctuary and probably celebrated some of their festivals within its mighty arches? Although some of the great sarsens might have fallen by 200 B.C., most of the damage to the final form was much later, when local people tried to break up the stones for building material. If most of the stones were upright then it would not have been difficult for wise priests to notice the significant dates when the sun and moon fitted so exactly in between the tall pillars. It does seem possible that the older celebrations on the solstices and equinoxes were continued.

The modern Druids trace their ancestry back to the beginning of the eighteenth century when learned people began to take an interest in arts and crafts, not only the artistic skills of painting and sculpture, but the more prosaic ones of masonry and capentry. Because skilled masons were allowed to travel freely to work on different building projects all over the country, and because written documents and trade unions were not then in existence, the masons had to have ways of recognising others skilled in their craft, hence the passwords and handshakes which were given to master masons and apprentices, and by which they could recognise each other. By 1717 men began to 'speculate' about such matters and to form lodges of 'speculative masons' who talked about the mysteries of the stonemasons' craft rather than actually carving stone. There was also room for the revitalisation of other ancient mystery cults. One of these was Druidry, and a new grove was created in the first quarter of the eighteenth century. Of course there was no archaeological evidence to support the concepts that were put forward, and even much of the literature on the subject, translated from Latin and Greek, was originally anti-Druid, but sufficient information was discovered to found a new Order. Because this was a secret organisation not a lot is known about the activities of these neo-Druids, but it is known that they began to hold ceremonies and celebrate the solar festivals. Initially these were in private, but at some later, comparatively recent date, the solstices and equinoxes began to be ceremoniously observed in public.

There are now at least three Orders of Druids in London, and each holds meetings to mark the solar dates. At the spring equinox, about 23 March, they may be seen on Tower Hill, for legend has it that the head of Bran (the Welsh name for the Sun God) was buried there to protect the country. King Arthur is alleged to have dug it up and ruled without such assistance. In the autumn Druids may be found on Primrose Hill, part of Hampstead Heath, holding the festival of Autumnal Equinox with due ceremony. The Golden Section Order of Druids performs its rites on Parliament Hill, one of the oldest gathering places about the capital which has not been obliterated by building. Here there is a tradition of free speech, dating back to long before the Romans came. Today there is a mixture of ritual performed by the initiates of the Order and their honoured guests, and a Gorsedd of music and poetry, out in the open. Later a feast of wine or cider and bread and fruit is shared among all comers. Sometimes elaborate maze patterns are marked out on the grass, for this has long been a part of the ritual tradition of the West, echoed in *Pilgrim's Progress* or Dante's *Divine Comedy*, where the seeker treads a winding path between this world and paradise, in the most simple terms.

At midsummer the Druids prepare for their third and final ceremony as the morning passes. The huge crowd which arrived for sunrise has often dispersed well before noon, especially when the festival happens to fall in midweek. Still there are the inflowing coach-loads of tourists from America and Germany who, when they discover the Druids in attendance, seem to think it is a show specially put on for them. The noon ritual is the longest of the three and may be closest to the original version. These days there are no offerings of virgins or even flowers to the Sun God, but there are processions and prayers, ritual gestures and a symbolic feast. Again the four elements are positioned outside the circle of arches, and these are collected by the white-robed column, led by the Sword-Bearer, his long, drawn sword held upright before the Arch Druid, to symbolise peace and protection. They walk sunwise round the monument until they reach the Hele Stone, where the sword is carefully lodged in a convenient crack and is then drawn by the Presider, an honoured companion, who re-enacts the task which made Arthur king, and united the people of his kingdom. Four officers then call for peace in the four quarters of the compass, and 'Peace throughout the whole world!'

The file of Druids, led by the Arch Druid and the banners of the Order, enters the sanctuary; the symbolic bread and wine, the flower and the smoking incense bowl are placed on a white altar cloth at the centre of the circle. Visitors from other organisations are welcomed, and three long poles of mystic colours are placed upon the ground in the form of the three rays of light which shine through the gateways between the stones at sunrise; this is the AWN or sacred word. A kind of musical hats is played with a great crown of oak leaves, which is offered to the Presider and then is passed round all the main participants. This symbolises equality, although 'some men are not equal in privilege . . .'.

After this, which should be at the moment of solar noon of the year, a rod is held upright and there is no shadow even if the sun is shining. 'It is time to celebrate the feast, in the face of the Sun, in the eye of Light, before all the people.' There are some more prayers and responses, followed by the reading of the scroll of the names of departed Druids, ancient and modern, which includes William Blake and many other poets as well as former chiefs of the Order. The bread and salt, the wine and the elements of fire and air are then blessed and offered to the Officers, and around the circle of companions. Later this consecrated feast is offered to all the audience, some of whom have no desire to be involved in a pagan feast; others participate in the true spirit of a celebration of the Light of the Sun upon earth, without which, after all, none of us would exist!

After the sharing of the bread and wine the Druid's Prayer is intoned; this does seem to be quite ancient and turns up in Breton, Welsh, Irish and even Cornish Druidic sources. In English it goes as follows:

> Grant, O God, Thy Protection,
> And in Protection, Strength,
> And in Strength, Understanding,
> And in Understanding, Knowledge,
> And in Knowledge, the Knowledge of Justice,
> And in the Knowledge of Justice, the Love of it,
> And in the Love of it, the Love of all Existences,
> And in the Love of all Existences, the Love of God and all Goodness.

The ceremony is nearly ended, and the Druids may seem to be wilting a bit by now, for they will have been keeping vigil and taking part in these summer celebrations for what seems like a week. They stand together rather like an advert for 'Gleamo' washing powder, in various shades of white, their nun-like Egyptian nemyss head-dresses fluttering, their long, ungirdled robes blowing round their feet, within this sacred enclosure where perhaps some sort of sun priests and priestesses have long held festival and kept watch over the changing skies. Long ago, on this very spot, they observed the setting and rising of sun and moon, marking their resting places with posts and later huge stones, patiently waiting for solstice and equinox, for eclipse and comet to pass above this lonely plain. Little has changed except now we have forgotten the phases of the moon, the tides of the year, and our festivals to celebrate these unaltered times are revivals, the ceremonies recently written and enacted in very different surroundings. But there are still folk who make this annual pilgrimage, who feel they have to be there to see if the sun will rise at its appointed time, to fit the framework of such ancient construction. Often they are disappointed when misty weather shrouds the horizon and the sun is not seen until long after dawn. Sometimes it rains, and black clouds hurtle across the endless skies like the Wild Hunt close behind its prey, the only light being diffused silver sparkles from dark zenith to grassy nadir. Nonetheless, to gamble on the English weather, to be there before dawn pales the eastern sky, to watch with bated breath those distant, white-clad Druids standing in the sanctuary of the sun as its light creeps over the black rim of the world, is an experience not to be missed.

There are no dancing girls, and little music except from the audience, although the Druids used to have a Celtic harp player; the processions are solemn and the proceedings strange, but there is an atmosphere of great antiquity, the feeling that the ghosts of other, earlier priests are there, only just invisible, waiting to see that the festival is kept, the sun rising in its proper place. If at dawn you seem to sense them, the unseen presences keeping vigil with you as the sky turns white and the stars fade from view, you will know that the eternal bond between earth and heaven has been renewed, that the promise of unity has been kept, and that the covenant between man and God will ensure the turning seasons beneath the eternal sky.

CHAPTER 6

Zulus, cowboys and Henry VIII's wives set fire to the Pope

> The finest rockets ever seen: they burst in stars of blue and green,
> Or after thunder golden showers came falling like a rain of flowers.
>
> *Epitaph to Gandalf,* J. R. R. Tolkien

> Remember, remember the fifth of November,
> With gunpowder, treason and plot.
> I see no reason why gunpowder treason
> Should ever be forgot.

It is a dark November night, the sky black and in part lit by a half moon, across which scudding wisps of light cloud drift against a background of stars. High up, within the confines of a small Sussex town, a dark angel with bronze-green wings reaches out over the heads of the people who have come to share the occasion. He is brightly lit and almost seems to glow against the black sky as he strives to lift off from earth into the soft, sea-tanged air. But it is not some heavenly being that the folk have gathered here to celebrate but rather the sacrifice of the living for the living. War and folly have caused the deaths of many and now, among other things, it is these deaths which are commemorated and life for which they were given. The angel arches upwards as a memorial to those who have died, and beneath his feet, around the monument on which he stands, the beginning of the festival of fire and disguise will occur.

Lewes is a hilly town, nestling in a valley among white chalk cliffs, yet far inland. From its quarries has come chalk which has made more acid soils fertile, and on the green pastures around, fine sheep and cattle browse between water-filled ditches in which herons stand guard, like feathered grey hock bottles among the sedges. The roads of the town support the idea of hills, for all of them seem to scramble up or swoop down from Town Hall to river, from War Memorial to shopping centre. Even the name of the place is derived from the Saxon word for 'hills'.

If you decide to participate in its Bonfire Festival then you would be well advised to come early, or park your car and come by train. Those from Brighton emerge from a tunnel through the chalk straight to the station which also lies at the bottom of some undulating streets. As you climb up towards the High Street you may well begin to sense the atmosphere of the coming event, for street traders are lying in wait for the revellers who are pouring into the town this chilly evening. Here and there hawkers with hydrogen-filled balloons ply their trade, and sellers of hot roasted chestnuts scent the air with their finger-singeing wares. There are flags and streamers, strangely green-glowing necklaces which light up the faces of the wearers with an eerie light, and many other sorts of trinkets by which to remember the occasion are offered to the quietly chatting throng. Along the streets, long since emptied of traffic, participants in the festival stroll to the gathering places of their respective groups. Plumes of feathers, sparkling tinsel on the various sorts of costumes are seen in the shadowy streets, but this is only a preliminary.

It is about 5.30 p.m. The sky is dark; sometimes the evening is mild and dry, in other years the sky will blur with that fine sort of Sussex drizzle which falls almost without dampening anything, but in any case the streets will soon be agleam. From the Town Hall to the War Memorial the pavements are crowded with local people and visitors; all the way down the hill and over the river bridge, there is an air of expectancy. Towards the bottom of the hill, where the great commemorative angel is illuminated by bright floodlights, the crowd is thickest, for under these lights the various troupes of celebrants will come, not only to pay their respects to the victims of wars, but also to remember their own seventeen Protestant martyrs who died at the stake in some other torchlit scene hundreds of years ago.

Loudspeaker vans drive through the cleared roadways as the people are pushed back by friendly police folk. 'This is a sad occasion,' says a metallic voice, recalling the horrors of war which many of the audience are far too young to have experienced for themselves. 'Many have made the greatest sacrifice and given up their lives that others may live. . . .' And live they do. Although the pubs are closed to all but the regulars, who creep in by the back doors, the crowds are cheerful for they are waiting for a spectacle rarely witnessed in these times. True, the television cameras are there, poking from an upstairs window in the glare of the floodlights, under the auspices of the angel. These mechanical eyes, and the long snouts of muffled microphones, will carry something of the scene and sound to viewers in other parts of the country. Most of the population of that part of Sussex is there to watch, or better still, to march in the processions.

The feeling of tense anticipation mounts to a climax, and a hush falls over the 30,000 to 40,000 folk who have come along for the event. The streets are cleared again, and the first procession makes its way down the hill to pay its homage to the dead and offer a sight for the living watchers. A local band, one of many, plays the 'Dead March from Saul', and the costumed marchers process solemnly down the hill. The strains of 'Last Post' echo between the tall houses, shops and banks in the square; there is a brief silence suddenly shattered by a fire-cracker. Then, against the glaring arc-lamps rises another light, golden and moving, flaring and windblown, as each marcher lights his or her torch. Suddenly the dark streets begin to glow with light, and the initial seriousness of the occasion gives way to elation. Smoke rises into the still air, smelling of hot paraffin and scorching cloth. Heat flares from each torch, and the crowds draw back as the procession returns up the hill. The band strikes up with 'Sussex by the Sea', and many an eye is wet, not only from the smoke and flares.

Each contingent of the procession has a particular theme, and each is led by one carrying a tall pole bearing a banner on which the name and motto of each group is painted. Above these signs are many flaming torches which flare and stream in the sea wind. Here there is a great mass of coal-black Zulus from Lewes's own Bonfire Society. Dressed in bizarre costumes of skins, bones and horns, with enormous head-dresses of wondrous feathery plumes, they march up and down the hilly streets of their town. Feathers of pinks and blues, yellows and greens, ostrich plumes and trailing imitation tiger tails, plastic skulls and golden ear-rings flash and glitter in the shifting light of the torches, sometimes held so close to the flammable feathers that it is a wonder that the wearer has not become his or her own funeral pyre. From the waving headgear 10 feet up to the mini-Zulus still in their prams below it is a great sight, and that is only the beginning.

Lewes 'Zulus' sport fantastic head-dresses of feathers and glittering jewels as they walk through the streets on Bonfire Night.

As if witch-doctors with bones through their noses are not enough, they are followed by contingents from other local towns and villages, interspersed with bands of Boys' Brigade pipers and drummers, brass or silver bands in smart uniforms, youngsters thrilled by the excitement of the evening yet still marching and playing their fifes and drums, their glockenspiels and trumpets. Because it is dark and it would not be easy for a musician to manage his instrument and hold a fiery torch, there is the added difficulty of being able to read the music as they march through the darkened streets. Some have solved the problem with miners' lamps, others have fastened electric torches to the tops of their instruments or the sides of their hats. Somehow every participant is determined to keep in step, play his or her instrument well, and read the music, come what may.

Next in the procession comes a Society whose 'Bonfire Boys' have taken the Western Trail, some in conventional cowboy attire, and others in sparkling, glittering sequined costumes designed for festival or Mardi Gras. Black hats, waistcoats, skirts

Dressed in Stuart costumes, a contingent of local folk carry their banner through Lewes on 5 November. (*Sussex Express & County Herald*)

and jeans are bespangled with shining ornaments which gleam and twinkle in the torchlight. Maybe these characters aren't as exotic as some but they glow in the darkness like the night-lights of some multicoloured city, and sparkle like Milky Ways of rainbow-coloured stars.

Behind them comes a mixed batch of historical characters, including King Henry VIII and all his wives, carrying torches which in their own day would have been commonplace. Here bright brocades and soft velvets glow in the wavering light, jewelled head-dresses and trailing silks waft and flutter as their wearers wander along the dark streets, chatting and smiling at the throng of watching folk. Here is a group of Cavaliers and their womenfolk in pale satin and lace seeming golden in the flaring flame-light. Rapiers shine, spurs chink on the paved way, silks rustle and hiss as they pass by under their own town banner. Some of Dickens's characters are here too, looking more modern, more familiar – and talking of which, witches and girls from St Trinian's carry their torches between the crowds. Watchers draw back from the heat of the flames as naughty girls – and probably lads as well – come by in short gymslips and long, black, holey stockings, into the garters of which are thrust catapults and pop-guns. Clubs and hockey-sticks are waved among the poles of torches, and the terrible mob goes on its way.

The Vikings may not have been to Sussex for quite a long time, but here they come. A ravening horde, at least a long-boatful, in hides and fur, armour and horned helmets, bearing great axes and swords. Inventive people, these twentieth-century Vikings, their breastplates seem to be scaled and plated with the debris of this metal age, for aluminium beer-can bottoms would hardly turn the edge of a two-handed man-axe – but look closer at that. Perhaps it is some other product of the computer age. Are those ear-rings of crafty, ancient design, or are they bits of technological hardware? Chains and mail glitter in the torchlight, damp fur can be smelled above the reeking, smoky torches. The procession pauses, and an old gentleman approaches a Viking warrior, mailed and mighty, his winged helmet and great buckler catching the light with gleams of copper and gold and iron, and asks for a light for a cigarette from the torch he carries. Peace and war, fear and friendship mingle here in the dark streets. The fierceness is, of course, pretend, and though small children may cower and clasp their mothers' knees as some spectacularly-costumed people pass, there are cries of glee and whoops of surprise once these characters are identified. To see real people in fantastic attire is very different from the same sight on television.

The air is thick with white smoke, heavy with the fumes of burning fuel, and tinged with the scent of hamburgers and hot dogs from the stalls of roadside vendors. The music from the brass bands is lost in the distance, and excited chatter from the crowds, interspersed with laughter and comments both kind and sarcastic about the costumes of the marchers in the Bonfire Society parades, ebbs and flows like waves on shingle. Now there is a different sound, the quiet jingle of small, silver bells mixed with thuds, cracks of wood on wood, and perhaps soft curses when wood meets flesh. Into the fluttering torchlight comes a small bunch of white-clad men, beribboned with bright colours and wearing straw hats decked with flowers. Accompanied by a fiddle-player and an accordionist, they are skipping in the long hey, the interwoven paces of the Morris Dance. Among the more sedate marchers their dancing steps and waving sticks, clashing together as they progress along the hilly road, make a sharp contrast to the walkers. With their traditional bells and garlands they bring a breath of the eternal returning sun of spring into this dark night on the verge of winter, and in their weaving patterns they dance the promise of life in this festival of death. The crack of their sticks and the tinkle of their bells traditionally signifies the bright forces driving out the evil spirits of winter and cold darkness.

In the procession, too, is the living Archbishop who presides over the revelries, and the effigies of the Pope and Guy Fawkes who are to burn in the bonfires at the end of the procession. Impressive though it may be, the torchlit marchpast is only one section of the evening's spectacle. Trundled behind the torch-bearers are the carts to collect the spent and smouldering torches from the gutters where they are thrown down. Safety is an important factor in this great happening.

The procession now stretches miles along the undulating road through the middle of Lewes. Contingents from Seaford, Rye, Uckfield, Shoreham, Buxted, Newhaven, Edenbridge, Crowborough and many other villages and towns join in the march. Costumes vary from the simple local pirates in striped jerseys and sea-boots to the expensive and lavish attire of the Siamese Dancers with sparkling, pagoda-shaped headwear, and tinkling bells around their ankles. Jewels and sequins shine and gleam in the fluttering torchlight, golds and silvers, lurex greens and

The effigies of the Pope and Guy Fawkes are carried in the torchlight procession to the Lewes bonfire. (*Homer Sykes*)

purples glitter in the dark. Cloth of gold gives way to feathers again as a group of Incas in full ceremonial regalia treks through this Sussex town. Make-up and costumes reflect the looks of these proud and ancient peoples. Torches flare and turn to smoke, the music of the bands fades below audibility, and the murmur of the crowd changes from admiration and exclamations of delight to more mundane subjects. 'What about a cup of tea, then, or some fish and chips, or a hot dog?' – the alluring smell of which is now more apparent as the guttering torches have moved away. The pubs are closed this festive eve, and travellers have to make do with non-alcoholic beverages, unless they have come prepared. The empty roadways soon fill with wanderers who seek to follow the Guy and the Pope to their symbolic immolation above the town, or watch fireworks from one of the lower bonfire gatherings on the flat river marshes. This great occasion is far from over even though the winding ribbon of yellow-orange flames has wound its way up and down the hills out of sight, as if some illuminated motorway had suddenly become mobile and set off into the hilly country round about.

As another factor of the procession, some of the Bonfire Societies have small portable set-pieces which are dragged along to the bridge over the River Ouse. Here the sputter and flare of fireworks announces the sort of spectacle that is to occur later on around the house-high bonfires up on the Cliffe and elsewhere. A flaming tar-barrel is carried on high to be cast into the waiting waters of the river, perhaps to signify the sun sinking behind the hills into its winter sleep.

To the ancient peoples fire was not only a symbol of the Sun God but of life itself. Each fire was a hope for survival in cold times when warmth could mean the difference between life and death. It is sad that the symbol of flames was degraded to become the executioner of heretics, especially as that very term is derived from the Greek word for choice. To choose not to follow some orthodoxy should not lead to a funeral pyre. The word 'bon-fire' may be derived from BON (French, good), or it may have come from the more gruesome meaning of bone-fire! To cremate the dead may be a reasonable idea, but to apply the same to the living is cruelty of the most parlous kind.

Bonfires are ancient gestures of defiance, and in placation to the Old Gods. In Celtic times fires were lit at Beltane (BEL = Sun God, TAN = fire, Celtic) and Samhain (summer's end, about the beginning of November). In spring the cattle were brought out of their winter quarters and driven between twin fires stoked with timber and medicinal and magical herbs, partly to ward off sickness and plague, partly to disperse those unseen evils which affected superstitious people, their kith and kin. At about Hallowe'en fires were lit to bring in the wanderers at the end of the summer, to reunite the families whose menfolk had been away at war or campaign, and to burn evil spirits and threaten them with loud noises. Now was the time when the excess cattle were slaughtered for salting down as winter food, for without hay and root crops it was not possible to keep large herds in wintertime. It was a time of feasting, for in the days before deep freezers and chemical preservation there were various bits of the carcasses which had to be eaten fresh. Feasts were prepared, not only for the living, but in many lands a seat of honour was left empty for the unseen guest – a representative of the folk who had died that year, or the God of the tribe, invited to attend and bless the feast and people. The richest and best of the meat and drink and bread were set out as an offering to ensure survival that winter, and plenty in the year to come.

There would probably be torchlight processions around the boundaries of the village to show the spirits which area was to be protected, and herbs of great potency would be burned among the logs. Folk would shout and make rough music with anything that came to hand, cooking-pots, the beating of spears on shields, hammers on ploughshares, knives on stones, drums and pipes to scare away sickness and starvation. Perhaps nuts and bones that burst with loud bangs would be added to the fire, anything to make a great commotion and avert future harm from flock and folk. Prayers and sacrifices would be offered to placate the wandering spirits of the dead lest they come and haunt the living by their fires in winter, or range over the hills, moaning and screeching in the wind, to frighten and freeze the cattle and sheep foraging in the scanty winter pastures.

Now we still have the bonfires, the crackle of bursting fireworks, the flares and flames, the excitement and the nocturnal torchlit processions, but the grimmer, more earthy matters have been forgotten or overlaid with more modern, up-to-date customs which apply to a mechanised age. We still have the guising, the dressing-up to avoid recognition by both friend and the unseen foe, the mummers' mimed and chanted plays in costumes of rags, the Green Man riding the boundaries like some ancient king assessing his realm, hidden in a cone of living greenery. We still honour holly and ivy and sacred mistletoe, that ancient 'golden bough', at Christmas time, and make garlands to hang on the door, as did our ancestors at their ancient festivals and feasts. Our reasons may be different; often we don't know for certain why we follow these traditions, but they continue nonetheless. It did not take until 1605 for there to be a need for a bonfire celebration; that was already established in the country folk's calendar.

Up and down the country there are bonfire celebrations, but at Lewes it is a fantastic fiesta, perhaps the nearest thing we have in England to the extravaganzas of the Mardi Gras, organised in the country world-renowned for its self-control and lack of emotional display; and here in this most genteel county of Sussex, probably best known as a place to retire to, or take sedate holidays by sea or downland, home of poets and subject of many of their most pastoral works, we suddenly find great celebrations.

Lewes' first bonfire was in 1557 when seventeen Protestant martyrs were put to death in the wake of the Marian persecutions. For the most part these were simple villagers who had tried to understand the scriptures for themselves, were regarded as heretics and so condemned to die – not a laudable act. Later, after the Gunpowder Plot in 1605 there was an occasion for bonfires to burn in celebration for the deliverance of Parliament, and so they did, upon the Cliffe at Lewes as in many other villages and towns throughout the land. By 1679 an effigy of the Pope was burned in Lewes, so starting the modern custom. Lads carried banners and dressed as Catholic clergy to add insult to injury, and finally cast the symbolic victim into a great fire late at night. By the middle of the next century the tradition was well established with fires and crackers and 'serpents' being added to the processions to add noise. Fires were caused to property in the town by some of these fireworks in 1795. By 1829 the burning tar-barrels had joined the flaming torches and fires, and now the tar-barrel became the symbol of a local magistrate who tangled with the Bonfire Boys on the bridge, and ended up in the River Ouse. Things got even more out of hand in 1841 when special constables appointed to try to prevent the procession got into a bit of a riot. A score of the celebrants ended up in jail that year. In 1842, perhaps as an alternative to riotous behaviour, bands of musicians were introduced. Relative peace reigned for a few years, but in 1847 over 150 local respectable tradesmen and inhabitants were sworn in on the side of Law and Order, but the Bonfire Boys got news of their gathering to plan protective measures and ambushed them in the town, by the light of burning tar-barrels. One hundred Metropolitan Police were called in as an added deterrent against the local Sussex lads, a number of whom were arrested during the fray that occurred. Lord Chichester read the Riot Act from the steps of the County Hall but this did nothing to end the fighting. Many of the London Police were injured, but the streets were eventually cleared.

The next year different tactics were tried. The whole affair was moved out of the town centre to the Wallands on the marsh, and there relative peace reigned for a year. In 1850 Pope Pius IX again brought England under the See of Rome; the Bonfire Boys were allowed back into the town, and they actually lit one of their fires

The Bonfire Bishop harangues the crowd before the lighting of the huge Cliffe bonfire. (*Homer Sykes*)

before the County Hall. The other, as from earliest times, was up on the Cliffe. Gradually the event took on a more peaceable appearance. Bonfire Boys processed through the town and the first Societies were formed, these being Cliffe and Town respectively, in 1853. By 1856 the first Bishop in clerical regalia had joined the procession with his attendants. Before the effigies were cast into the flames the Lord Bishop gave his sermon to the gathered people. A new effigy joined the Pope and Guy Fawkes one year when a miscreant made off with the money collected by the marchers; he was symbolically burned the following year as a threat of what might happen if he tried again.

At the turn of the century the Bonfire Boys managed quite quietly; a few were arrested in 1906, but were acquitted and

formed another Bonfire Society with its gathering in Commercial Square. During the First World War there were no activities, but Cliffe began again in 1919. It carried on despite difficulties and opposition of various sorts up to 1939, when war again put paid to these festivities. After the war things began again with a great muster in 1945, and continue to the present day. Each year the Societies excel themselves in originality and scope of their costumes and set-pieces.

Each Society plans its costume theme months beforehand, and has Fancy Dress parties and judging either before the Great Processions or earlier in the year. They also plan the form and design of the great set-pieces and tableaux which they will present at the bonfire itself. This is shrouded in the greatest secrecy, for though the name of the piece may be well known locally, only the select few, sworn to silence in the late summer, are aware of the details. The huge design is planned even to the

Flaming torches light up the standard of the Cliffe Bonfire Society as the costumed revellers march on 5 November at Lewes.

CLIFFE
LEWES

smallest firework, and it is carefully built in flammable materials so that the pattern of rockets and thunder-flashes will fire at the exact intended moment. Crackers and jumping-jacks are placed to lead runnels of flame about the form of the masterpiece when it is set on fire. All this preparation continues under a pall of security which would make M.I.5 blush.

If you follow the procession up into the hills to join one of the six groups which have their own bonfires or huge, elaborate set-pieces of fireworks, you will discover the next part of the evening's entertainment. It is here that the Archbishop of the night comes into his own. Banners have declared 'Down with Popery' and many slogans are aimed at one of the Popes during whose reign the Protestant martyrs died in this land.

Those who have the stamina may choose to follow the Bonfire Boys of the Cliffe Bonfire Society with their vast emblem of the times which will be dragged up the hill, harangued and finally committed to the flames among exploding, inbuilt crackers. Up on the Cliffe there is a high, grassy (and in wet weather very slippery) bank from which to watch the next part of the proceedings. It is here that the matters of national or international dispute are argued, and the Bonfire Bishop makes his speech, against a background of exploding rockets and Roman candles. In the darkness, as the great bulk of the bonfire waits to be consumed by bright flames, the last part of the ceremony begins. When the great effigy of symbolic design has been hauled up to the right place, speeches are made against 'Popery' rather than the current incumbent of the Throne of Peter, and the traditional Guy is harangued by the mob. Now the flames catch on the huge fire, built with skill and care to burn well, and across the dark sky rockets fling scattered stars of red and silver, gold and green. The crowds roar, and one by one the anti-hero of the Gunpowder Plot, and the immense symbolic design of the year are put to the flames and utterly destroyed to yells and heckling from all participants in this incredibly ancient festival of fire in winter.

All around fireworks burst with clouds of coloured sparks, rockets screech above the watching faces, shooting out meteors of white and red and blue fire, thunder-flashes rock the night with deafening bangs, showers of golden rain and silver waterfalls glitter against the dark. Volleys of lights zoom across the windy heights above the Cliffe. The last of the effigies to be immolated in a fiery furnace is the Pope, to jeers and yells from the crowds. Gradually the figure is consumed by the flames, yet

A magnificent burst of fireworks traces patterns of lights across the November sky. (*Sussex Express & County Herald*)

the hand raised in a blessing gesture seems to resist the fire and hovers, illuminated as a sign of forgiveness and benediction. Soon there is nothing left but the roaring flames and the soaring fireworks and pyrotechnic displays. In the distance the rockets of the other fires and gatherings may be faintly seen, but the great festival of light in darkness, remembrance of death in war, death in flames and death of the summer, which is surely the oldest part of this celebration, is coming to an end. Rocket sticks scatter the landscape, bonfires fall into embers, and charred, bright wood dulls to pale ash as the night draws on. The last smoky brands sizzle out and darkness enfolds tired folk, their eyes bleary with smoke, their necks stiff with the effort of following the progress of rockets across the sky, their feet weary with tramping the streets and hills of Lewes. The glittering costumes will be taken off and carefully put away until next year, the feathers wrapped in tissue, the sparkling lamés laid to rest in polythene. It has been a great festival, but next year it might be even more spectacular.

CHAPTER 7

St George fights a Turkish knight on Boxing Day

Please to help the Guisers, Please to open your door,
Please to give the players an apple from your store,
Please to help the Guisers, please to let them in,
Please to help the Guisers, and join their merry din.

Christmas is a festival season with dozens of customs, some individual to one family and others of great significance to a large proportion of the Christian population of England. Even the date of Christmas, 25 December, was the time of the pagan feast *Dies Natalis Invicti Solis,* the birthday of the Unconquered Sun, originally Mithras, a Persian Sun God who was born this day in a cave. He grew up as a warrior God who reluctantly slew the bull with a dagger, and from its blood came forth all manner of good things. In the carvings of Mithras there are often many of the Zodiac creatures, the Lion and the Scorpion as well as the bull and Man of the four fixed signs. These recur, slightly varied as the Four Gospel creatures of Matthew, Mark, Luke and John, when the Scorpion has become an Eagle.

Although it was Prince Albert who introduced the decorated tree into the Victorian living-room at Christmas, a tree decked with tinsel or flowers or ribbons has been an ancient symbol of plenty, perhaps in its cruder guise as fertility, since time immemorial. The Green Man, or Jack-in-the-Green, which we may recognise now as the name of a pub, was originally the centre of the spring festival, for someone was dressed in a great cone of light basketwork into which green branches and flowers were woven, and this character danced or rode a horse through the village or fields to bring luck and plenty to all who saw him. He was a more recent depiction of the Green Man whose foliate head with leaves instead of hair, or twigs issuing from his mouth, can be found in many a church and cathedral. On roof boss and

Jack-in-the-Green, the old pagan God of Fertility is often seen on inn signs all over the country. (*Brian Shuel*)

misericord, on pew end and font, the Green Man peers out upon the congregation, reminding some of the spirit in growing things which was worshipped in its own rite in earlier times. The cloisters at Canterbury have dozens of variations; Winchester and Salisbury, too, have their foliate faces, peeping from the stonework. Most old churches were probably built by masons whose craft is very ancient, who knew about the spirit of luck and life, and incorporated his face here and there in the fabric of the Christian edifice they were building.

One plant which doesn't often get into church with the Christmas greenery is mistletoe, the Golden Bough of Sir James Frazer's enormous work on folk customs and survivals from all over the world. In England the Druid priests gathered this mystical parasite from apple trees (sacred in their own way as the Tree of Immortality, before being the Tree of Knowledge). The branch had to be cut without using steel or iron (probably with a sickle of bronze polished golden for the occasion), by someone of great purity. It was not allowed to fall to the ground but was caught in a white linen cloth. Sometimes a white bull was sacrificed at this midwinter rite, so the older Yuletide feast would have been beef. The green leaves which showed life on the otherwise barren winter trees again relate to that life spirit, and the white berries were considered symbols of the seed of the Sun God, giver of life to all green things.

What is often not known is that when kissing under the mistletoe bough the lad was expected to eat one of the non-poisonous berries to bring him virility and lots of children. Most of the mistletoe seen here at Christmastide comes from Brittany where it grows in the cider orchards and is easier to reach than the great clumps which can be seen at the top of the tall limes in Bushey Park or Hampton Court grounds, among other places. Of course, it does grow on the Somerset apple trees in the Isle of Avalon, resting place, maybe, of the Once and Future King. Though it is rare on oak trees in this part of the world, a different, larger variety grows on the evergreen oak in Greece. Mistletoe is known as the 'All-Heal', and even now it is used in herbal medicine. Researchers are trying to discover its particular healing alkaloid.

Another old Saxon custom which is tending to die out with the advent of central heating, is the burning of the Yule Log, or in the West Country the Ashen Faggot. In past times a huge tree root, to burn longest, was hauled into the hall with singing and dancing, and piled into the centre of the great open fire, to bring light and warmth to the whole household for the Yuletide season. The great log would be kindled with a cinder from the last year's log, to ensure continuity of life to the land and luck to all the folk. Nowadays we can only remember this item of the midwinter festival with a log made of Swiss roll, covered with chocolate icing and topped with an edible festive robin. This symbolism of the ancient custom has crept across the Channel from France.

In medieval times the beast of the feast was not the fairly modern turkey (introduced in the sixteenth century), but a whole sucking pig, garnished with herbs and spices; or, for the poorer folk, a haunch of the family pig, killed in the depths of winter and roasted before the open fire on a spit. It would be accompanied by plum porridge, a cross between beef broth and Christmas pudding, when dried fruits, meat and fat were all boiled up into a thick soup. Mince pies were common too, but they did contain minced meat as well as the candied fruits, peel and suet of the modern variety, cooked in a 'coffyn of paste' or pastry shell.

Mulled ale, made in those pointed copper gadgets often seen shining in pub bars, was a good winter drink, when ale was spiced with cloves and cinnamon and ginger, and the copper muller was stuck in the fire to warm up, its contents then being poured into pewter tankards and supped round the fire. Another traditional old Christmas drink which would surely perplex the barmaid at the Holly Bush, is 'Lambswool'. This is a heady concoction of real cider (which, like real ale, is made by small firms), the pulp of roast apples, sugar, nutmeg and ginger stirred up well. The apple froths up like the fleece of a lamb, hence the name. However, it may have originally been a harvest speciality, for its Celtic name is LAMASABHAL (= Lammas-tide apple), and Lammas is now at the beginning of August, so last year's apples would be pretty ripe – and this year's only small windfalls. Sometimes it was part of the Feast of Samhain, or Hallowe'en, at summer's end. This is another custom that deserves revival.

Singing of carols before Christmas by groups of youngsters who carry lighted candle-lanterns and knock on doors, seems to have been replaced by lorries with loudspeakers, driven by people collecting for larger charities, or lads with tape-recorded choirs knocking up households when collecting for their own presents. The idea of singing special songs at each festival time is another ancient tradition which is found all the year round and all over the world. Christmas carols began to bridge the gap between sacred and secular songs, for they were often sung in the vernacular, and though they had holy words the tunes were often gay, lilting familiar ones used by the folk about their business in field and farm, town and village. 'The first Nowell . . .' – from the same root as news, which ties up with Gospel, in Old English 'God spel' – good news, bringing the announcement of the Redeemer's birth; 'Adeste Fideles' ('O come, all ye faithful . . .'), and many others. 'Silent Night . . .', the German carol, and the traditional 'Holly and the Ivy . . .' which may be one of the oldest, for its words may have been altered from a pagan original. There used to be May Day carols and harvest ones, but the name commonly now means a song at Christmastide.

Once the great glut of Christmas dinner is over and the television has lulled the well-fed family to peaceful slumber, once the seasonal cake has been cut at tea-time, the tree stripped of its goodies, and the whole place is a-rustle with discarded wrapping papers, Christmas Day draws to a close. This, of course, is not the end of the festival by any means. In the old days the feast lasted for 12 whole days until 6 January, now seldom remembered in any way except that it is unlucky to leave the decorations and cards up any longer. Also, the holly and the ivy, those symbolic plants which have been tied up with pagan practices for thousands of years, are cast into the fire, often to the detriment of the chimney as dried holly burns like tallow. The greenery, which represents the spirit of growth and the new year of the sun, is cast out because the days are growing imperceptibly longer, albeit much colder, in January, but the power of the sun is being restored; light, and thus life, will return to the land.

What has brought about this happening? Today we accept that the power of the sun waxes and wanes as does the moon because of the Earth's path around the sun on its annual journey. We do not need to pray to a spirit in the sky that warmth and growth may return; we know that by the time the new television series has got under way we will find snowdrops and crocuses in the gardens, and soon the first of the winter daffodils will thrust forth their golden and orange and white trumpets among deep green spears, and spring will be on the way. No one gets up in special costumes and makes sacrifices to the Sun God, or begs the Lady of Spring to return to her people nowadays – or do they? Well, if you happen to be in Surrey, or Gloucestershire, or one of the other places scattered around England where this custom is preserved, or perhaps has been recently revived, then you may witness a very old festival, probably on Boxing Day.

At Claygate, a small, suburban village not far from the main commuter railway line to the south-west of London, the old festival of midwinter is celebrated in a traditional way. It begins outside a pub, as do many of these customs which involve men, for ale to them is the elixir of life, and what better time to quaff deep and celebrate? Boxing Day was the old time when servants would go to their masters carrying a box with a slot in it, or craft apprentices would have one made of clay, sometimes square, sometimes in the form of a pig – hence piggy-bank – into which money could be put, and except by skulduggery with a thin knife, could not be extracted until the box was broken open or the pottery pig sacrificed to the hammer. Then all who were entitled to draw on the box could share and be sure of their portion. 'Please, Sir, to remember the Box', the man or maidservant would say, though often they were given a present of clothing on the day after Christmas – through which they had no doubt worked morning, noon and night! The box was for those from outside who served the house – the butchers, bakers and candlestick-makers would make their contribution.

At Claygate, outside the 'Foley Arms', a Young's house (Morris Men prefer real ale), at about opening time on Boxing Day, you will find a gathering of folk. If it is pouring with rain, or snowing, most of them will be inside, but the weather tends to be kind to the Morris, for theirs is natural magic, and it seldom rains on the dancers! They will be having a jar to wet their whistles and oil the joints before they begin the serious matter of the day. These are the Thames Valley Morris Men who have come forth from their Christmas jollity to share with any who watch the luck which is their gift by right. Or perhaps one should say that they dispense it to those spectators who are generous when the collecting box comes round. Morris is mostly done for fun these days, but the dancers are worthy of their hire, and they can offer good fortune like the gipsies, although the payment they will exact is much smaller. Toss a coin to the Morris, pay your offering at midwinter to the Gods who created the Gods, or for the upkeep of an old tradition, it doesn't matter which, and buy a share of luck.

Dressed in white, with hats of straw covered with ribbons, real or plastic flowers, badges of places where they have danced and so on, with bells about their knees, they come to dance first; then they move on to the next pub in this tour, and perform something tied up with this season of the year. Because it is early, and cold, they dance still wearing their waistcoats. Each man has one, lovingly made by his wife or girl-friend, blue as a midsummer sky and decorated on the back with a tree of all sorts of colours, designs and methods of embroidery, but always depicting the dancing legs as the trunk of the tree. This is the Tree of Life in one of its myriad interpretations. Each jacket is original, and they are only worn by the main side; the 'prentices have to dance a while before they earn the right to wear the full uniform. They have to shiver in white shirts and blue and yellow crossbelts, and between dances take refuge in anoraks and other more prosaic attire.

The 'Foley Arms' is the home and start of this Boxing Day meeting, but it is not the only pub which is part of this particular dance-tour. Once the dancers have quaffed the odd pint of Young's they are ready to move on to the next pub which gets its beer in red barrels, but there beside the trunk of a now defunct

Morris dancers are nearly always accompanied by fiddle or accordion music and the drinking of real ale.

oak tree of considerable girth, the dancers fulfil yet another part of the meaning of their association. This is another facet of the life out of death theme, frequently disguised, overlooked or forgotten, but underlying many of the ancient customs and festivities. Here the Thames Valley Morris have gathered to perform a mumming play, a local Surrey version of one used as a Pace-Egging play derived from further north or west.

The Folk Play has had a number of forms and probably came originally from a semi-religious text which over the centuries has been simplified and changed to a light-hearted representation of the battle between life and death, summer and winter, and so on, the eternal opposites which strive for domination or at least balance. Here the dancers make a space among the throng of Boxing Day watchers who have been dragged from their firesides this chilly morn, on the pretext of exercise and fresh air, or because they happen to enjoy Morris dancing and/or beer! By now, noon, a fair crowd has gathered and the Whiffler, or Morris Squire has to clear a space for the Guisers to play out their action. The idea of disguise is very old, for Boxing Day is a time for asking for gratuities from employers, or begging from the general public. In the old days this was frowned upon, so faces were blackened (Black-a-moors – Moorish – Morris goes one theory of the derivation of the name), or the characters were dressed in shreds of cloth or paper, as they still are in Gloucestershire, so that no one could be recognised. Another reason for hiding their faces was because the dancers represent Good; their play and dance is an attack on evil or darkness, so they were masked in order that the opposition, visible or otherwise, would not know them and cause harm or bad luck to befall.

Once space has been made – 'Room, room, gallons of room . . .' – and perhaps a few notes have been played just to soften up the audience for the entertainment that follows, the actors in this strange survival come into the ring of expectant watchers, in all manner of strange gear. When they have lined up they will shout or sing something after the following lines:

> The door is open, we enter in, your fear or favour for to win.
> Whether we stand or whether we fall, we'll do our best to please you all . . . .
> If you can't believe what we say, step in, St George, and clear the way . . .

There are many versions of the whole thing and each group learns it from another, so words and characters vary from play to play – all part of the fun. St George in armour, with a sword and a shield bearing his red cross on white, introduces himself:

> Here comes I, St George, a knight of courage bold,
> If any Saracen is near, I'll make his blood run cold.
> I fought the evil dragon and brought him to the slaughter,
> And that is how I won the King of Egypt's daughter.
> Where is the foe that bids me stand? – I'll cut him down with my right hand!

This challenge has to be met, and the character variously known as Bold Slasher, the Turkish Knight, or the Blackamoor, brandishes a huge scimitar and announces himself with:

> Here comes I, Bold Slasher, a Turkish Knight,
> Come from a distant land to fight,
> My body is made of iron, my head is made of steel,
> My hands are made of beaten brass – no man can make me feel . . .

There is a fight with lots of overacting and wild swordplay but eventually, encouraged by the audience, St George strikes down his adversary. The Whiffler, or sometimes Hobby Horse (the old-fashioned sort with the horse's head and body, and a real-looking rider with his feet in stirrups, played by a good dancer), calls upon the watchers for a Doctor to revive the corpse. Sometimes he claims to be the Turk's father, but calls: 'Is there a Doctor can be found who can heal this deathly wound?' Enter the Doctor in top hat and tail coat (at Claygate he had a shower-fitting by way of a stethoscope), and of course the black bag. Again there are all sorts of claims made as to his abilities to cure '. . . the itch, the stitch, the palsy, the gout, the ills within and the ills without . . .'. He takes various items from his bag and finally a little bottle of the Elixir, which he administers to the Turkish Knight who, after a bit more hamming, scrambles to his feet. 'Arise, Bold Slasher, and play thy part.'

Next to come on the scene is Beelzebub:

Here comes I, Beelzebub, over my shoulder I carries my club,
In my hand is a frying-pan – am I not a jolly old man?

Sometimes he is another attacker of St George and again is slain and revived by the Doctor; sometimes he is followed by Little Devil Doubt with a sweeping broom, come to drive people into hell or death. These two are primarily there to assist with the extraction of money from the audience, the Devil threatening, Beelzebub proffering his pan, or sometimes a ladle, to be filled with coins. Sometimes there is a Betty, a Man/Woman who may be the Doctor's wife, or simply a stand-in for the female principle which is not otherwise seen in the play, especially as women don't take part in this tradition.

Because of the season of festivities the figure of Father Christmas comes into some plays:

In comes I, old Father Christmas, welcome or welcome not,
I hope old Father Christmas will never be forgot.

He does not fight but generally helps with the collection of money from the crowd. No one is expected to give a large sum, but every

The Thames Valley Morris Men's Hobby Horse swallows a coin offered by a small onlooker. (*Thames Valley Morris Men*)

silver coin is welcome, tossed over the heads of the crowd or thrust into the Morris Men's box.

This sort of folk play is very lively and the spectators are expected to cheer or jeer the characters as the story is unravelled. The Turk may be booed or harangued, the victorious St George cheered, and of course the doctor with his reviving potion, often hawked like some English medicine show: 'I have a notion that this very potion will cure all the sick and return to the quick even the dead . . .' and so on. There are lots of different versions of the characters, but no matter who fights whom, or what the main contenders are called, there is always the doctor among the cast to revitalise the slain; sometimes one, often several victims need his healing attention.

When the play has ended and the Morris Men continue their journey to the next pub, they are back again in dancing attire and perform in the car park of 'The Winning Horse' along the road. The bells jangle and the sticks thwack, the handkerchiefs flutter as they work through the figures of the 'Shepherds' Hey', 'Lads-a-bunchum', 'Beansetting', 'Rigs O'Marlow', and 'Step-an-fetch-her'. The accordion sings, chilly watchers stamp their feet in time, and small children peer enthralled through the legs of their elders. People who have never tried any of the seemingly simple steps and movements chat about what fun it must be to gather and dance and drink beer, entertained for the moment by the colours and gestures of the dancers, but not involved in the significance of Morris.

No one seems to know whence came the idea for such things as the Mumming Play, although its obvious antecedents include both the religious mystery play and the secular sword dance. In some versions of the latter the leader of the team, or the Fool in some areas, places his head in the centre of the lock of swords; these are suddenly withdrawn, it seeming to the audience that a real sacrifice has been made by beheading, as the character drops to the ground. This has been linked with pre-Classical times when ritual dances to the pagan gods actually ended with a real sacrifice of one of the dancers, perhaps chosen by lot, or the one who happened to be in the correct place at the time. Dancing was very much involved in ancient religious practices, and even the Old Testament tells how David danced before the Lord. In Greece the performances of plays in the vast amphitheatres were in part religious and partly secular, and they had dancing sequences.

The Fool, who plays an important part in the Mumming Play (*P. Haveland, A.R.P.S.*)

The name 'Morris' has sometimes been attributed to 'Moorish' in that the steps and movements were imported after the Crusades, and the fact that some accounts of dancers mention that their faces were blackened. Morris sides don't do this now, although the Bacup Britannia Coconut Dancers do when they perform their curious dance around Eastertide, with nut-shaped bobbins in their hands and tied to their knees. Another suggestion is that this survival of religious/magical dancing is in honour of the Virgin and so these are Mary's Men, dancing dressed in white and coloured ribbons in honour of the Mother of God, who has always been the Mother of God, before Jesus came to earth. She is the White Goddess, Lady of Spring, remembered at Christmas as the fairy on the top of the tree, on May Day as the Queen of the May, at harvest as the Corn Dolly, and as the Hag at Hallowe'en. At this time of Trick-or-Treat games it is the children who dress up and play pranks on their elders or, carrying turnip lanterns, beg small gifts or sweets.

Another possibility is *Mores* dancers, that is those who adhere to the *mores* (Latin, customs) of the place, and so they are performing traditional dances for fertility and luck, for spring after winter, and for protection from evil. The new king of some societies was chosen by a contest with his rival at about the time of solar midnight, the winter solstice around 21 December. The same idea is reflected in the medieval tale of Gawain and the Green Knight. Gawain cut off the Green Knight's head (a clear reference to the old God of Nature), but afterwards the Green Knight picked up his head and booked the return match for the following year, much to Gawain's consternation. When the time came, because of his bravely presenting himself for apparent execution the Green Knight struck him a token blow on the neck and fulfilled the bond. This is another pseudo-sacrifice, such as occurs in the Mumming Play.

The sword dance, now found particularly in Northumberland where each team numbers five dancers, has a different history from the Scottish dance with a solo performer nimbly leaping over crossed sword and scabbard (which may have developed from the Morris Bacca Pipes Jig). This is a fast tripping step where the members of the team are linked together by the short, whippy, two-handled swords and caper through intricate movements, tapping their feet and whirling in a tiny, tight circle. A good team is supposed to be able to dance on a bar top without falling off. There are often several extra characters, similar to those of the Mumming Play, the Fool and the Man/Woman Betty, who encourage the dancers to harder and more complicated figures. 'This figure cannot be done!' cries the Fool as the men perform it, and then they surge inwards, lock their swords into the magical five-pointed star, to be carried off by the leader. This Rapper Sword dancing is now found mostly in mining areas, although the six-men teams of the Longsword Dance are found further south, and the lock of six swords is often seen as the

A cake with a sword thrust through it and garlanded with flowers is offered to the crowd to bring luck and plenty by the Thames Valley Morris Men on Boxing Day.

badge of the English Folk Dance and Song Society. Perhaps the thudding feet and the clashing swords were intended to arouse the spirit of spring to return after the winter withdrawal of the sun.

Some of the Mumming Plays are called 'Pace-Egg Plays' and are named after the Pasch or Easter Egg, so this ties up the idea with spring rather than midwinter. In Cheshire, Soulers act the story at Hallowe'en (All Souls' Eve), and beg Soul Cakes in repayment. There is a Soul Cake song, rather like the Hot Cross Bun, 'one a penny, two a penny' Easter ditty. The Celtic year ended at about the time of Hallowe'en, and again the new year would be celebrated and its luck worked for within the magic of the men's dance.

The actual history of the play is very old, probably deriving from the morality plays of the Middle Ages, which in turn stem from the religious dramas which began as a simple representation of the scene at the tomb of Jesus, after the Crucifixion. At first the priests merely acted out the arrival of the Three Marys and the angel telling them that Christ had risen. Other bits of Biblical drama were added, and this gradually developed into the miracle plays which were pushed out of the Church, first into the porch and then into the street, where they were taken up by guild members into the pageants of the Wakefield and York cycles. From these came the morality plays which, instead of acting out Bible stories, portrayed the idea of the battle between good and evil, with the characters called Life and Death, Everyman and Time – not real people but concepts. From the Evil One came the Mummers' Beelzebub whose club shows him to be an earlier folk hero, in the steps of Hercules, or the great giant Helleth, the white hill-figure at Cerne Abbas whose oakleaf-shaped cudgel links him with the Green Man. The Fool, too, is a representation not of folly, but of wisdom in disguise. Consider the Fool in *King Lear*, or Malachy, the Starved Fool whose prophecy concerning the Popes is still making sense. There is a reversal of roles; the Devil becomes Beelzebub who is more of a buffoon than a force of darkness.

The play seems to have developed from an intervention by the Betty during a sword lock when 'she' is accidentally executed, and the Doctor is called to revive 'her'. Gradually more characters were added and the actual dance faded, and because this was based on the priestly religious drama mixed with the early stage plays where boys played all the female parts (hence all the dressing-up and sex-changes in Shakespeare, etc.), women never took part in the Morris nor in the Mumming Play. There certainly must have been women's magical and ceremonial dances, but these may have been solo, or shared only with the immediate family, and danced indoors out of sight of the others. The men's dances are concerned with the Sun, so perhaps the women danced for the Moon, whose waxing and waning phases ruled their lives and bodies.

However, to a great extent, it is due to women that the Morris survived, for many of the young men who knew the dances were killed in the First World War. It was only because some of their womenfolk remembered the tunes, and the steps that had been danced by the men, that the tradition could be carried on. The dances were taught to a few lads after the war, and Cecil Sharp, who collected folk songs and dances, helped with the preservation of this folk tradition. The English Folk Dance and Song Society's headquarters in London is named after him, and houses a fine library, and a shop selling all manner of musical instruments, books, badges, and all the appurtenances of Morris and Folk dance. Some of the best male dancers today were taught by women who had remembered the old steps and movements.

Not all Morris sides have the Mumming Play or its equivalent, nor do all sides go in for sword and rapper dances, although all forms of Morris are gaining popularity and many unlikely places have teams – even Croydon has the Northwood Men, who wear green and yellow crossbelts, and their symbol is an acorn. Mumming is said to be a corruption of miming or silent acting, as in the phrase 'to keep mum', but there may be some other derivation. Anyway, it is one of the oldest forms of folk play still being acted, and is well worth getting out on a cold winter's day to witness.

CHAPTER 8

Apples, eggs, corn dollies and a burning ship

> To everything there is a season, and a time to every purpose under Heaven. A time to be born, a time to die. . . . A time to weep, a time to laugh, a time to mourn, a time to dance. . . .
>
> *Ecclesiastes 3 : 1–4*

Almost as soon as the last of the Christmas decorations have been cast on to the fire, or the surviving glass ornaments and tangled fairy lights consigned to their summer abode, some people, particularly in rural, cider-making areas will be getting ready for another celebration.

Once again in Somerset, although they do something similar in Kent, a bunch of folk will be preparing to go wassailing. Now many people think that wassailing is carol-singing, and I suppose it is, in one sense, but it has an older, and in this context, slightly different meaning. On the evening of 17 January (old Twelfth Night, to those who recall the change in the calendar) a group of people prepares another activity concerned with warding off harm and ensuring peace and plenty, this time among the orchards of apple trees. In some places it is the villagers, in others Morris Dancers have taken on this task, but basically it is similar. The idea is to go out this bitter winter night with barrels of cider, guns, and toast, and sing a song to an apple tree! Like many festivals it seems totally irrational, although there may run through it a thread of logic.

A short, torchlit procession goes out into the orchard at Carhampton in Somerset; the participants are dressed in a sort of

Local farmers with shotguns and Morris Men with mugs of cider 'wassail' (bless) the apple trees on a bleak January evening.

medieval costume, and carry a huge tankard full of cider. Under an old orchard tree they all pause and sing:

> Here's to thee, old apple tree,
> Whence thou may'st bud and whence thou may'st blow;
> Hats full, caps full, bushel basket, sacks full,
> And all my pockets full, too. Hooray!

The slices of toast are dipped in cider and stuck up among the branches, shotguns are fired upwards through the trees to drive off evil spirits, libations are poured over the roots, and drink is shared by all the carollers, who may dance about the trees, or shout and sing to bring fertility and good luck.

Under these trees we have again a confluence of several streams of tradition running together. Wassailing dates back to the Vikings, the greeting given in *Beowulf* being 'Waes thu hal'. The Saxons would offer a guest a cup of ale, saying 'Was Hail', roughly translated as 'I wish you good health' (as in 'hale and hearty') 'and good luck'. The guest would reply 'Drinc Hail' – 'I drink, and good luck be to you'. This custom of drinking each other's health on Twelfth Night from a Wassail Bowl, decked with ribbons and containing mead spiced with sweet herbs, or a sort of punch, was well established by the fourteenth century. Initially this was indoors but later it was taken out into the open, and Wassail Bowls were carried about the streets. 'Here we come a-wassailing, among the leaves so green . . .' although sung at Christmas may be more appropriate to another time of year for it continues: ' . . . God bless you and send you a happy new year' – which could equally apply to the new growth of plants.

The apple tree is traditionally one of the candidates for the Tree of Knowledge of Good and Evil in the Garden of Eden. Eve offers Adam an apple, and his understanding is broadened once he tastes it. As well as imparting knowledge this sacred fruit was considered in Welsh mythology to be the key to the Otherworld, and with a branch of apple blossom Bran the Sun God ventured into the land of the Everliving, and the branch guaranteed his return to his own place. Cut an apple in half crossways and discover its secret, a symbol which occurs all over the place in religious and mystical pictures.

Apples turn up in Hallowe'en games as an indication of immortality, for you are trying to seize the magic fruit from under water, or from a string hung from the ceiling, as if you were snatching a fragment of life from the darkness. At the start of November when summer has definitely faded and the dread, cold hand of winter strips the gold and green from the face of the land, there is a pause while folk adapt to the winter season. Now lots are cast, omens read to see what the dark tide has to offer; sometimes there are fancy dress parties featuring witches and wizards, goblins and demons among the chosen costumes. These days it is all in fun, but in times past it was a season of great fear and trepidation.

The next festival which is celebrated all over the Christian world is Easter, originally the festival of Eostre, the Goddess of Spring. As well as the religious celebration when the Redeemer returned to life, again showing the symbolic power of Light over darkness, it has always been the time when the rebirth of nature is demonstrating the return of the sun out of winter's icy grip. In London there are great parades of decorated floats, folk in fancy dress, vintage cars, bands playing modern and marching music, and great throngs of people turning out to see the splendour.

The two main symbols which turn up at this festival, which is still set by the phase of the moon, rather than being a fixed date in the calendar like Christmas, are the egg and the Easter bunny. The egg is a fairly obvious symbol for spring, for the chick which comes forth is a little golden promise of the bird that is to be, as the weak yellow spring sun is a forerunner of the hot gold sphere of the midsummer blaze. There are all the yellow spring flowers, daffodils, forsythia, crocus in gardens, coltsfoot, primroses, and gorse which is always in flower somewhere (when gorse is out of flower, kissing is out of season!), glimmering in dull green winter foliage like tiny suns cast down upon the land. As these flowers blossom brighter with the lengthening days they seem to show the sun how brightly to shine.

Eggs are offered as gifts; in earlier times they were ordinary hens' eggs, dyed or painted with plant colours, and offered to pagan shrines. Now they are replaced with edible chocolate eggs, decorated with coloured foil and packed in bright boxes. This is the eternal symbol of life reborn from something which looks inert and lifeless, as nature is reborn from the dead branches of trees, the barren, dark fields which now mist with slender green spears of newborn wheat and barley.

The Easter Bunny is a different symbol, not a bunny rabbit at all but a hare, sacred to the Moon Goddess. March hares dance and fight in the fervour of their mating courtship in the dusk, and seem to be celebrating the return of life in the light of the spring moon. Hares were taboo, and seldom eaten in England except on festive occasions; even now, as with horse-flesh, a few people eat hare as a general dish, and for much the same reason. The horse and the hare were sacred to the White Goddess, and hares were hunted in Her honour at the Spring Festival. Hares were also magical creatures, for witches were supposed to be able to adopt their form when attending moonlit meetings in desolate places. Was it just for camouflage that participants in lunar rites pretended to act as hares, leaping and prancing against the full moon, so that distant watchers mistook their dancing silhouettes for wild animals, or could they actually shape-shift into the creatures themselves?

All the festivals of March, April and May are designed to encourage the young sun to shine brightly and dispel the dismal days of winter, to bring back green life which is the food source for livestock and people. Demons are driven out with fires and shouting, loud noises and offerings of eggs and flowers. Local customs vary because of what has been remembered, revived or started. Sometimes there are processions, sometimes fancy dress, or costumes of leaves and flowers are worn by the participants. New clothes are put on for the first time, bright colours emerge in field and hedgerow. Wild flowers turn from the yellows of spring to the blues of bluebells, speedwell, harebells, scabious, reflecting the azure vault of the heavens, mixed with white blossoms of windflowers, blackthorn and whitethorn, elder in creamy bunches like the head of a pint of ale. Pinks and mauves appear as the days grow longer and the hay harvest gets under way. Towards midsummer the bright red corn poppies and scarlet pimpernel – the poor man's weather vane – glow like fires in cornland verges. The wheel of the seasons continues its slow, eternal revolution, and daily the sun climbs higher into the heavens, its power and strength increasing.

At this time many villages would get their share of good luck by dancing round the maypole on the village greens. In some Kentish and Sussex villages the custom is still kept, usually towards the end of May or even early June, when there are plenty of flowers. Traditionally, there is the May Queen, chosen from the pupils at one of the junior schools, who is crowned and decked out in a long white cloak and carries a garland of flowers. Usually she has a number of attendants, even a May King in some places, although it really is her day. She (though she may well not be aware of it) is a representation of the White Goddess, the Earth Mother in her Maiden aspect. In ancient times there was a sacred festival with the Spring Queen and the Corn King, who went into the fields and by their own mating, made them fertile. The ordinary folk would spend the night before the feast in the woods, gathering green branches and flowers to deck a bower for the Queen and King, among other things! When the dancers circle the maypole with its coloured ribbons and bright flower crown they are celebrating the very force of life, and magically binding it into their land. Sometimes after this dance everyone would go out into the fields with garlanded sticks or broomhandles covered in flowers and leap high, singing and dancing, to make the corn grow tall, and the beasts become fertile. Today we have forgotten our pagan past and rely on artificial fertilisers in plastic sacks to make our crops successful. The older way was certainly more fun!

In the sunset glow of a warm June evening, many cars may be seen moving slowly along certain seldom-used Cornish lanes. Some of the drivers will occasionally stop outside an isolated farm and go to ask directions, but most have made this particular journey in previous years, and know exactly where they are going. It is 23 June, and people of the Helston area are flocking to Manhay Farm in the old parish of Wendron, where as darkness falls a great bonfire will be kindled. This will be but one in a chain of beacons throughout the 80-odd miles of the Cornish peninsula, a living strand of fire stretching from Chapel Carn Brea near Land's End, to Kit Hill near the Devon border.

The Midsummer Eve Bonfire celebrations were revived in 1929 by the Federation of Old Cornwall Societies, which has been responsible for the rescue and maintenance of many of Cornwall's lapsed customs, including Helston's Hal-an-Tow folk play. At the time of writing there are thirty-nine member-societies, many of which organise bonfires in their respective areas. The Redruth O.C.S., for instance, builds the beacon on Carn Brea (not to be confused with Chapel Carn Brea, whose bonfire is usually the first to be lit), and the Truro O.C.S. lights a fire at Four Burrows. One of the most prominent bonfires blazes on the top of St Agnes Beacon which overlooks Cornwall's rugged North Coast, and which is reputed to have been the stronghold of the Giant Bolster.

As with so many ancient customs, this is one which was Christianised by the early fathers, and so it is also the Feast of St

John. A local clergyman will offer Christian prayers and, around some of the fires, a local band will supply the accompaniment to the singing of Christian hymns . . . but behind and beneath these renderings runs the thread of pagan ritual that was enacted at the lighting of the Baal-fires. This is accentuated when the prayers are repeated in the Cornish language. At Helston's fire this is usually performed by the current Grand Bard of the Cornish Gorsedd, standing in amity alongside his Christian counterpart.

If we join the line of vehicles heading for Manhay Farm on 23 June, we shall eventually turn through a wide gate into a field where already many cars are neatly parked. The regular attendees of this annual ceremony are probably wearing gumboots, for cattle habitually browse here, and after dark it is not easy to avoid the underfoot evidence of their presence! The wellie-wearers are clad in warm garments, too, for as night falls it will grow damply chilly beyond the zone of heat generated by the bonfire. For the same reason it is wise to bring a flask of hot tea or coffee.

This field of Mr Harvey's farm is set on a kind of plateau from which one has a splendid view to all parts of the horizon. To the south can be seen the lights of the Royal Naval Air Station at Culdrose, and later, if the night is clear and starry, one might also be able to see, flickering in the north, the light of the beacon on Carn Brea. Scattered around the field are plenty of handy boulders on which to spread a rug and sit, and just behind the great, waiting stack of brushwood, gorse and empty cardboard boxes, is a strange subterranean chamber. This is the remains of an ancient tomb, called in these parts a quoit. The huge capstone is scarred by a long crack; evidently at some time an attempt was made to break up the stone for modern building purposes, but it resisted the effort and was left in place, making a fine vantage point for some of the many children here tonight.

Here comes the band, moving through the deepening blue shadows of dusk to group itself near the towering, flammable pile. Some years it will be the Wendron Silver Band which sets the night air throbbing with assiduously practised music. On other occasions the musicians will make their way here from Gweek, where Ken Jones cares for his seals, and where the inhabitants are probably still talking about the recent summer when a large group of touring Morris Men performed nobly in the yard alongside 'The Gweek Inn'.

After a few preliminary puffs and oompahs, the band launches itself into its first offering. To the vast amusement of the audience, most of Mr Harvey's cows immediately hasten to the stone hedge which keeps them pent in the neighbouring field. Resting their bovine chins on top of the hedge, they swish their tails and seem to be enjoying the music as much as the humans.

By the time the band has run through its repertoire, it is almost full dark. A few streaks of rosy light in the far western sky bear mute witness to the 'descent' of the Sun, to whom the coming fiery ritual was originally dedicated – and still is, in a modern way. For, after the singing of a hymn – 'Praise the Lord! Ye Heavens adore Him' – the President of the Helston O.C.S. steps forward and gives an explanation of the ceremony. This, of course, is mainly for the benefit of new members of the O.C.S., and holiday visitors from 'up-country', of whom there are surprisingly many. Nevertheless it is strangely impressive even to ears which have heard it before – the account of how the ancient Celts of this land – and probably pre-Celts as well – paid tribute to the Sun God at this time of year, the zenith of his fiery power. Then the attentive audience hears of the coming of the new faith to Britain, and the wisdom of its early propagators who sought not to obliterate paganism entirely, but to adapt its rites and festivals to serve the new religion. Thus the Midsummer Eve fire-festival became the Feast of the Nativity of St John the Baptist.

Next comes the prayer for the Benediction of the Bonfire, spoken first in English, the current language of the 'new' faith, then in Cornish, the tongue (however modified by a lapse of nearly 200 years and its subsequent revival) of the old Celtic Sun-worshippers. (From now on this ceremony will include no further mention of St John!) There follows an open acknowledgement of the pagan origin of this rite, when the Master of Ceremonies announces: 'According to the custom of our forefathers in days of old, behold us making our Midsummer Bonfire this night in the middle of summer.' The pagan theme is underlined by the next participant, the Lady of the Flowers. Whether young, middle-aged or elderly, whether costumed or in ordinary clothes, she is obviously representative of the Earth Mother, the Great Goddess who shared with the deities of Sun and Moon and Sea, the homage of the ancient peoples. Bearing her beribboned sheaf of flowers and herbs, she steps forward to the unlit stack, saying:

In one bunch together bound,
Flowers for burning here are found,
Both good and ill;
Thousandfold let good seed spring,
Wicked weeds, fast withering,
Let this fire kill.

Then she repeats these lines in Cornish, which she may have learned at evening classes, or perhaps she has been carefully coached to pronounce the words phonetically. The M.C. bids her cast the flowers on to the stack, and again the instruction is repeated in Cornish.

Once the sacrificial bouquet has been tossed on to its woody altar, the long-awaited moment of kindling is at hand. This symbolic act is usually performed by a local dignitary; in the present case it might well be the Mayor or Mayoress of Helston. Other beacons will be lit by the Chairman of a Parish Council, or perhaps a well-known businessman or professional person of the particular locality. No matter whose the hand, it receives from the M.C. a flaring torch, gleaming and streaming in the chill night air. In a strong, carrying voice, the Fire-Lighter proclaims:

I set the pyre at once on fire;
Let flame aspire over many a parish.

Then, as if speaking directly to those aforementioned ancestors, he cries the same thing in Cornish:

Tan y'n cunys, gorraf desempys;
Re splanno an tansys dres lyes plu.

And the stack, carefully constructed by Mr Harvey and his helpers, receives the torch and wakes to crackling, roaring life.

A great cheer goes up from the assembled spectators, then the band strikes up for the final hymn. This is usually 'God, that madest earth and Heaven', a plea for protection during the sunless hours of night. During the singing of this hymn, many eyes watch the fiery death of the flower-offering, and many folk probably wonder about the significance of the plants used in the bouquet. Ideally it should consist of at least nine different varieties of flower and herb and, as specified by the Lady, some must be 'good', some 'ill'. The 'good' plants include some of known medicinal value, as well as others once reputed to afford protection from evil influences. Since this is the Feast of St John, the principal benign plant is the golden, star-shaped St John's Wort, which Welsh people call the Blessed Plant. Another herb which has been long sought for its cleansing properties is vervain, used in times past to sweep the altars of the old gods. The list from which to choose is long, and includes rowan and oak, valerian and elecampane, foxglove and sage, yarrow and clover.

As for the 'bad' herbs, perhaps it is inevitable that the list should begin with the four weeds of man's first curse, viz. bramble, thistle, dock and nettle. These are followed by three considered to be the farmer's bane: tormentil, cinquefoil and rest-harrow.

When a balanced selection has been made, the plants are carefully bound with ribbons of five different colours, each colour being significant of a particular quality. White is for strength, green for wisdom, blue stands for love, red for sacrifice, and yellow is symbolical of the Sun, for whom this bonfire rite is enacted.

After the singing of the final hymn, the bandsmen (and women, and sometimes even children) leave the site, and the provision of music is taken over by a folk group. While they settle themselves close to the bonfire, tuning their instruments and deciding what they will play, many of the spectators are queueing up at the rear of an estate car from which is emanating the mouth-watering scent of hot Cornish pasties. Others have brought their own comestibles, to be washed down with the contents of flasks or cider-bottles. The atmosphere relaxes from its earlier solemnity; the hot, glowing light of the great fire illumines smiling faces and skipping children, and casts smoke and shadows over small groups of folk who are perhaps meeting each other for the first time since last year's ceremony. The sparks fling themselves skyward as if attempting to join their star-brothers, and the light southerly breeze sends a long plume of dark smoke towards the distant flicker of light that is Carn Brea's bonfire.

The folk musicians, slim, dark figures silhouetted against the flames, gather up willing voices to roar out the choruses of old and well-loved country songs. 'Goin' up Camborne Hill, comin' down' is a steady favourite of Cornish folk clubs and pubs, and commemorates the first pasenger-carrying journey of Richard

Trevithick's steam locomotive in 1801. 'The Old Grey Duck', 'Sweet Nightingale', and 'The Tree on the Hill' (also known as 'The Rattling Bog'!) are also likely to get an airing this night, and perhaps the singers will even render that grim declaration of Cornish rebellion, 'The Song of the Western Men':

> . . . And shall Trelawny die?
> Here's twenty thousand Cornishmen will know the reason why!

The origin of this particular song is something of a mystery. The tune is very much like that of the old nursery rhyme, 'The Grand Old Duke of York', and has been adapted in Cornwall not only to miners' songs, but also for Christmas Mummers:

> Oh, a-mumming we will go, will go,
> Oh, a-mumming we will go,
> With bright cockades all in our hats
> We'll make a gallant show.

Some authorities aver that the Trelawny referred to was the Bishop of Bristol and later Exeter, who was committed to the Tower of London in 1688. Others insist that he was Bishop Trelawny's grandfather, imprisoned in the Tower for contempt of the House of Commons in the reign of Charles I. Whatever the truth of the matter, it would appear that the Trelawny line was ever aggressively vociferous in the cause of Cornish autonomy!

Slowly the fire sinks to a mass of glowing ash and charred sticks. Parents gather up their children, switch on their torches and pick their cautious way through the cow-pats to their cars. The grass is wet with dew and night-mist, and one's breath clouds the midnight air. The summer solstice is over, and from now on the days will shorten as the sun rides daily lower in the sky. Perhaps some of the folk now moving away from Manhay will remember this night as they listen to the moan of winter winds, and will recall the strange, wild joy engendered by the witnessing of this ancient fire-festival. The following poem won a 'Highly Commended' certificate in the literary competitions of the 1976 Cornish Gorsedd. Written by one who was then a member of the Helston O.C.S., it seeks to encompass all the solemnity, joyousness and mystical antiquity of this revived midsummer rite.

Fire on Manhay Beacon

There was a kind of madness in the air:
not the terrifying dark
of mind-slaying insanity,
but a wild and joyous idiocy,
dancing in every flame-flung spark,
and stretching smiles on all the faces there.
Spreading smoke scarfed the sky,
a great, smudged finger pointing east,
seeking to link with smoke of sister-fires
on Agnes Beacon, Four Burrows and Carn Brea.
A quiet, nacreous mist
crept from the cooling earth to lie
around the feet of those who served the pyres
and watched the paler dying of the day.
And there was music: old hymns, folk-songs;
light and laughter, warmth and linkèd hands,
Benediction, spoken in the old tongue
of Kernow, fey and deep-mysterious land.
Four elements awoke the ancient power:
nocturnal mist gave moisture to the grass;
air fed the blaze; then, in the final hour,
fire bowed to earth, surrendered and passed.
Midsummer midnight. Nothing moves but time.
Black now the beacons, no more smoke to climb
upward and eastward from high places where,
earlier, there'd been sweet madness in the air.

Beryl M. Mercer

Another old custom revived by the Federation of O.C.S. takes place at harvest-time, and is known as 'Crying the Neck'. Once again we have a Christian thanksgiving ceremony superimposed upon an older, pagan tradition. One evening in late August there will be a 'muster' of O.C. Societies in a suitable field of some Cornish farm. A field of golden stubble, for 'all is safely gathered in' – all? No, not quite, for in the centre of the field, surrounded by a circle of straw bales which provide seating for the spectators, is one lone stook of corn.

The Master of Ceremonies – usually the President or Hon. Sec. of the host O.C.S. – carries out a roll-call of the other Societies present, and bids them welcome. This is followed by the singing of the same hymn which opens the Bonfire celebrations, accompanied by the music of a local band, and then the M.C. explains the history of the ceremony.

It seems that in ancient times neighbouring Cornish farmers would compete against each other in friendly rivalry to see who would be the first to finish the reaping. (One aspect of this contest has remained unchanged to the present day: as well as trying to outdo each other they were, of course, racing against the weather.) As the winner slashed free the final sheaf he would raise it high, and shout to the four points of the compass: 'I have'n!' Back would come the cry: 'What 'ave ee?' – and in triumph he would reply: 'A Neck! Hurrah!'

From this final stook would be made the traditional Corn Dolly, hung in the barn or farm kitchen to ensure a good harvest for the next year. However, the slowest competitor, the last farmer to complete his reaping, would view the coming year with some dread, as it was considered an omen of ill-luck to be last.

As at the Midsummer Eve Bonfire, a prayer of thanksgiving and benediction is offered by a local clergyman, then repeated in Cornish, after which the farmer whose field this is proceeds to cut and bind the lone stook. The watchers admire his easy expertise; then, as he lifts the sheaf, they draw breath to make the responses. He raises the golden bundle to the north, and the ancient harvest litany begins:

'I have'n! I have'n! I have'n!'
'What 'ave ee? What 'ave ee? What 'ave ee?'
'A Neck! A Neck! A Neck!'
'Hurrah!'

This is repeated around the horizon, an extra 'Hurrah!' being added each time. After the flushed, grinning farmer has been suitably applauded, it is the turn of the Cornish speaker, who repeats the calls in the ancient tongue of this land:

'Yma genef! Yma genef! Yma genef!' (literally, 'It is with me.')
'Pandr'us genes? Pandr'us genes? Pandr'us genes?' (literally, 'What is with you?')
'Pen Yar! Pen Yar! Pen Yar!'
'Houra!'

Now there is a peculiar anomaly here, for *pen yar* does *not* mean 'a neck', it means 'a hen's (or chicken's) head'. It seems possible

Two woven Corn Dollies, representing the Earth Mother and a traditional Horn of Plenty guard the corn spirit until the new sowing.

that the pagan ritual demanded a blood-sacrifice to the Earth Mother; perhaps after the last stook was cut and carried away to be used in the creation of the Corn Dolly, image of the Goddess, a farm bird was killed in the field and its blood allowed to soak into the stubbled earth. Whether or not this actually happened, the Cornish version of the call seems to retain a trace-memory of something older and darker than the simple harvest thanksgiving offered up in modern, rural churches.

However, in *The Golden Bough* Sir James Frazer traces back these old harvest cries to those chanted by early Egyptian reapers, which in turn revert to the rites of Osiris. Frazer sees the last stook as the neck of the Corn Spirit, 'who is consequently beheaded when the bunch is cut down' (Ch. 47, *Lityerses*), and he goes on to quote examples of this custom from many rural parts of the British Isles and the Continent. In some cases the 'neck' becomes the 'tail' – of a hare, cat or fox. Only in Dumbartonshire is it called the 'head', and we are not told to whom or what this head belonged.

After the calls have been uttered in Cornish, thus paying lip-service to the Old Gods of Cornwall, the 'new' faith reasserts itself with another hymn:

> This is the field, the world below, in which the sowers come to sow:
> Jesus the wheat, Satan the tares, for so the word of truth declares;
> And soon the reaping time will come, and angels shout the Harvest Home.

This is the conclusion of the open-air part of the ceremony; the farmer is warmly thanked for the use of his land, and for his part in the proceedings, and then the crowds begin to disperse. Most will adjourn to the nearest church for a short service (taken by the reverend who attended the ritual), which will include the well-known harvest hymn, 'We plough the fields and scatter the good seed on the land . . .' After this they will no doubt be more than ready for a welcome Pasty Supper.

As the sunset light reddens the stripped cornfields, coaches will carry home those Societies which have mustered from other parts of the county, their members replete, happy – and perhaps a little pensive, too. They have witnessed one more facet of ancient ritual, one more revived tradition of their forefathers who ploughed and sowed, tended and reaped these fields centuries ago, paying their ceremonial dues to the deities of the land that fed them.

The harvest festivals in churches have been celebrated, usually about the first week in October, and the vast marrows, globular green and red apples, sheaves of corn and other produce have been redistributed and the Harvest Supper shared among parishioners. 'All is safely gathered in . . .' echoes in town and village throughout the land. Today the harvesters are skilled technicians who master the complicated combine harvesters which roam the fields of ripe corn like scarlet prehistoric monsters, spewing from their mouths into attendant lorries the golden grain, very different from the scene of our grandfathers' time. Then, everyone in the village had some part in the reaping, by hand with sharp sickles, working in lines across the sun-scorched fields; everyone was involved and it was their harvest.

In November there are two more public festivals, one very

small but interesting, the other larger and more dramatic. On 5 November in Shebbear, a small village in the back lanes of Devon, there is a festival which has nothing to do with bonfires, but with a boulder, a great, flat, reddish rock, chucked down by the Devil on one of his flights from Hell to torment the people of Earth. At the foot of an oak tree, outside the gate of the small, square-towered church, it squats. As evening falls on 5 November the bellringers stir the darkening air with changes and peals on their six bells. The villagers gather, possibly in the pub called 'The Devil's Stone', to build up their strength and prepare for the strange local custom.

The evil spirits will have been stirred up by the bell-ringing when a team of stout local lads, armed with poles and crowbars and led by the vicar, sets about its annual task by torchlight. They have to shift this hefty rock and turn it over, as folk have done for hundreds of years, to ensure prosperity and luck. Compared to some of the big festivals this is a very short and simple affair. There are no special costumes, no traditional song telling a complex tale; folk aren't very sure as to why this old custom is maintained, yet like many other local ceremonies it is kept up by a handful of people feeling that if they don't roll the rock every year near the date of old Hallowe'en, ill-luck may befall, or in this agricultural area, crops or stock fertility may fail. Having had a few jars they prepare to shift this boulder, a ton or so of oval-shaped, foxy-red stone, lying there beneath its tree just outside the consecrated boundaries of the church. There is no helpful Department of the Environment notice to explain, so perhaps it is just an erratic boulder, left by some earth upheaval or vagrant glacier long ago. Someone got the notion into his head that it might be fun or advantageous to turn it over, just for luck, and so it is done.

Perhaps it is one of those soft, inland Devon nights when a gentle breeze whispers through the oak's branches. Are watching eyes peering from the holes in its trunk, ghostly hands rattling its winter-turning leaves, eerie voices murmuring directions to the lads who are to perform the action? Torchlight reflects off the grey stone of the wall of the cottage behind as the participants get ready to lever and heave and shove, cursing softly (the vicar is there!), in rumbling Devon accents. Poles are thrust under the smooth edge of the stone, hefty shoulders hunch to take the strain, corded muscles clench, crowbars creak, and gradually – oh, so slowly – this russet rock is heaved up on

The villagers of Shebbear in Devon turn the Devil's Stone over each 5 November in order to drive harm away. (*Homer Sykes*)

edge. It teeters, then with a thud and a muffled cheer from the participants it tumbles over. Watching the effort required to shift this stone, weighing about a ton, one wonders how much muscle or mind power was needed to raise the Grey Wethers, those sarsen sheep of the Kennet Downs, into the pattern and accuracy of the Stonehenge circle.

Perhaps the Devil's Stone was originally a boundary marker, for there are plenty of places where 'Beating the Bounds' is still carried out, when the choirboys walk the boundaries of the parish, striking the stone and other markers with long willow rods. In some places one of their number is gently bumped, head down on the boundary stone, or dangled into a cruciform hole dug nearby, as a symbolic sacrifice or offering. A different boy or girl is used for each one as you can't offer second-hand victims! Is the Devil's Stone something like that, and does turning it over on its small patch of grass beside the tree and the village square, ensure peace and plenty for the handful of inhabitants? Perhaps it marks a ley line or the site of some older ritual. Whatever its meaning or origin, this custom has been kept up for a very long time. Maybe you could call in at the 'Devil's Stone Inn' and ask them about it. When the torches go out, and the boulder has been turned over and replaced in its hollow out of the way of cars parked for church services, the local folk are content that the proper thing has been done.

In Rye, again in Sussex, not too far from Lewes, there is another Bonfire Festival. This has been revived recently after a bit of a break, for as well as the procession of brightly costumed torch-bearers, they have motorised floats snaking through the twisty, hilly streets of the place. Rye is a coastal town the sea abandoned. It feels as if, when you look over its walls or peer between the old houses, set on cobbled streets or twisting lanes which seem too narrow for cars, that the sea should be there, lapping about its feet, and that sea-going fishing boats should bob and ripple at their moorings, but there is a sinuous river and no waves.

Here the bonfire celebrations take place later than in Lewes, perhaps by a fortnight or so, and if it was wet at Lewes it may be dry at Rye. There is more wind here in the narrow lanes, and the costumed marchers who begin at about 5.30 p.m. carry their fluttering, streaming flambeaux at arms' length. Again some of the fantastic costumes of Lewes are here, for Bonfire Boys from many villages and towns send in their colourful contingents. Here we have the local carnival queen, warmly wrapped in a furry cloak as she rides in a sporty car among the marchers.

Here, too, there are several local bands with silver and brass instruments to play jolly music against the wind, and a jazz band has also joined the procession to provide an alternative to the rather sedate oompahs of the brass bands. Within the winding column small, brightly dressed drum majorettes in red and white and blue, with warm cloaks and twinkling batons, strut and cavort among the older marchers, the plumes on their smart caps nodding in time to their dancing footsteps. They look so pretty and so proud, as watching mums and dads crane over the bunched spectators, or follow behind with coats and wrappers for when they stop at the bottom of the town. School-fellows wave and point as they flutter past like tiny, mobile windmills with shiny, silver whirling sails.

One of the decorated floats which roll through the twisting streets of Rye, Sussex, in the procession towards the great Burning Ship (*R. Swettenham*)

As they disappear round a bend the roar of the engines of lumbering lorry floats drowns the music of the bands. The local W.I. has put on a good show of costumes on the back of a small van; this year it is 'London Street-Cries', all appropriately dressed and decorated. One of the pubs has decked out a large trailer with a copy of a medieval inn scene, and it is hard to tell from the lusty singing, beating on the bar-top, and dancing among the straw on the floor of the mocked-up tavern, how much is due to the ale served by comely wenches from the large barrels on the bar. A condensed circus follows on the next float with a gorilla, a ring-master (or -mistress, in topper and fishnet tights); clowns and trapeze artists swing and balance as the trailer lurches and weaves its way down the winding, hilly lane. Other lorries with merry crews represent local business interests and various carnival themes. Of course, this is not like the many large processions and carnivals found in daylight in towns and villages all round the country, when huge numbers of spruced and polished vans and trucks display their colourful loads, to advertise local firms and interests.

Here at Rye they are just a side-show to the real activities. They do add spice to an interesting evening and are greeted by an enthusiastic audience, but they really help to lead the watchers away from the sheltered, maze-like streets, to draw forth the more wary indoor types from around their firesides and television. Alas, even the bars of the charming 'Mermaid Inn' are closed this festive evening, and the cosy nooks and ancient, panelled rooms of this old tavern are empty, except perhaps for wily residents who have bespoke their beds and dinners. Men, women and children clatter and natter down the cobbled lanes, following the elusive sound of the bands, caught and lost among the leaning cottages and narrow shops. Down the hill all are drawn, out on to the marsh, on land where the sea used to be, for here is the sacrificial victim of this Bonfire Night.

Rye folk are united in one great party, one great sending of blossoming flames and arching rockets, screaming upwards in the dark. They have a different centre-piece though, for the Rye Bonfire Society sets fire to a ship. Not a real old coble or defunct dinghy, or a decrepit fishing smack, ex-property of the Ancient Mariner, but a great ship with sails and rigging, cunningly constructed by experts. Once all the folk have filtered downwards from the town and gathered in the flat lands below, there are a few speeches, lost in the wind. Torches sputter out, and the hot dog scents waft about the scene, ice-creams are clutched in winter-mittened hands; large and small watchers surge and wander to see this ship immolated in fire, its wrong element and all the more dramatic for that.

A local worthy is responsible for seeing that this galleon of packing crates and cardboard, about the size of the *Santa Maria* in which Columbus sailed the ocean blue, is set on fire to roar scarlet and yellow in a jet black sky. A small flame flowers, bangers crackle within, a rope of the rigging catches fire and, like a string of flags, flames rush upwards below a cloud of white smoke. The outline of this ship is dark, and shadows of watchers are silhouetted as fire catches and the shape turns from black to glowing, surging golden light. The form is there as heat drives back the audience to form an enthralled and open-mouthed circle which slowly enlarges as they back away from the raging inferno. It retains its ship-shape, its masts still stand even as the sails are devoured, and the phantom figures of guys or dolls on deck redden and char below the blazing rigging.

It is a fascinating, horrifying spectacle as this fine ship on an ocean of dark grass flares and founders in a welter of flying sparks and charcoal railings. If this were the funeral rite of some antique king it could hardly be more spectacular, more filled with awe and heat and roaring flames. The skilled fireship builders have succeeded again in ensuring that this recently revived custom goes off to a most dramatic and hellish finish, and as the gold and crimson ashes tumble into a shapeless pile, eyes are drawn upwards again to stare as silver and gold sparkles mark glowing rainbows in the sky. Showers of white and green and blue make imaginary waterfalls, Roman candles explode with fountains of red and purple stars. Volcanic fireworks spill glowing lava in gem-like rivers from carefully designed set-pieces. Catherine wheels spin, dizzying the eyes, and special rockets leap howling into the moonless night. Clusters and fans and cloudbursts of brilliant fire whiten the sky, and glowing spent sticks thud softly beyond the sea of rapt, upturned faces, as one after another these man-made shooting stars and comets zoom like multicoloured meteorites across the face of heaven. The last sparks fall, the shipwreck fire diminishes, and flames and lights desert the sky, leaving it once more bejewelled by stars of older make.

CHAPTER 9

Giant men and beasts and forgotten feasts

> The nine men's morris is fill'd up with mud, and the quaint mazes on the wanton green for lack of tread, are indistinguishable. . . .
>
> TITANIA, *A Midsummer Night's Dream*

On a steep hillside in Dorset, in the middle of a rather coffin-shaped field a tall man is standing. He is quite thin and you can see his ribs. In his right hand he carries a huge club and has a slightly surprised expression on his face. He is completely naked and extremely virile and his grass green skin matches the turf on the hill around him. He has been watching, brandishing his oak-leaf-shaped club for maybe thousands of years for he is Helith, the great Cerne Abbas Giant. No one knows when this great figure was carefully cut from the grassy slope, turves being removed to expose the glistening white chalk only a few inches below. Above his head there is a rectangular enclosure of banks and ditches which might have just been a cattle pound or could have been a small sacred enclosure.

Helith was for a long time regarded as a fertility symbol and a maypole was set up above him so that the local lads and lasses could weave the patterns of coloured ribbons which bind the power of the sun to the earth. Perhaps the tripping dancers with their bright streamers in some way copy the patterns of the moving stars and planets, circling and arching across the sky. Sometimes the ribbons are woven under and over to form a tight tent, like a wigwam crowned with a garland of flowers. Other dances make a delicate spider's web of reds and blues and yellows, the girls dancing one way and the boys the other, yet twirling round each other at every meeting. Like the spiral dance at Helston Furry, some sort of natural force is drawn in by the winding up of the dancing column and its fecundating power linked to the local landscape.

At Cerne Abbas barren women were able to call upon the Giant's virility by spending a night on his huge green phallus, when the moon was new, and asking for his aid in getting with child. The custom was continued for hundreds of years and must have given many childless wives hope for a family, for in order that such a custom continue to be observed, it must have been successful often enough.

One thing that is strange about Cerne Abbas is the fact that this is church village, Cerne of the Abbots. The Giant is obviously pagan, was certainly there long before the local monastery, yet he was not covered over or even altered to become some great green Christian saint. Perhaps the monks were wise enough to recognise that Cerne was a protective spirit with his mace. Cerne may tie up with Kern, the name of the corn dolly which is carefully woven from the stalks of corn in the last sheaf to be cut from the field. In the plaited stems, tied with red ribbon to symbolise life, the spirit of the harvest was kept by the farm-house hearth, in a place of honour throughout the winter so that the new wheat or barley would spring up one hundredfold after the next sowing. Cerne/Kern may be a representation of this corn or fertility spirit.

It is also possible that he was associated with Herne the Hunter, the leader of the Wild Hunt, which in Celtic mythology roamed the skies in storm clouds, the music of the hounds being echoed in distant thunder. He, too, is a representation of the old god known as Woden in Norse Myth as well as being called *Gwyn ap Nudd* (Light born of Night) in the West Country. Here there is a link with Glastonbury Tor, which was said to be the castle of Gwyn ap Nudd. One of the early Christian saints was invited to visit his underground castle, and was finally persuaded to accept after three requests. On entering the fairy king's palace and seeing its treasures, he cast Holy Water about himself and everything vanished, leaving the saint, his sacred duty done, alone on the bare Tor.

If he is indeed a hunter god he may well tie in with the antlered figure depicted in a bas relief on the Gundestrup Cauldron, a great silver bowl, discovered in Denmark. This beautifully decorated cauldron shows a god figure, sitting cross-legged, wearing a sort of tight-fitting knitted suit and holding a serpent in

Helith, the Cerne Abbas Giant, is clearly a Green Man associated with fertility. The enclosure above used to have a maypole erected in the spring. (*Aerofilms*)

his hand. He is crowned with antlers, and from the Celtic title of the Horned One, is called 'Cernunnos'. In some inscriptions this same horned/hunter god is called 'Cernenus' which is very close to Cerne, the name of the village where his figure is seen. As a Celtic god he had some of the attributes of Jupiter, so was associated with thunder, he was also the Lord of the Animals.

In a Welsh legend there was a supernatural being with a huge club who, after striking a stag until it bellowed thus calling all other creatures to it, had them kneel in homage to him. Although the Cerne Giant does not appear to have any horns or antlers it is possible these were marked on the original form. He certainly may have been carrying a cloak or net over his left arm, for this has been seen in aerial photographs, although it is not visible from the ground.

Helith may also be a Western version of Hercules who also wielded a great club and performed twelve labours. That seems to link him with the twelve signs of the Zodiac, and with other Sun heroes. There is a carving of Hercules found at the delightful-sounding Roman town of *Corstopitum* (Corbridge) in Northumberland which is very like the naked Dorset giant, brandishing his club. Hercules also was associated with a serpent which harks back to the Gundestrup cauldron's antlered deity with his ram-headed serpent. As Dion Fortune says in *The Sea Priestess*, 'All Gods are one God, and all Goddesses are one Goddess, and there is one Initiator.'

If he is the hunter then he may be Herne, who turns up in Windsor Great Park, perhaps watching over the Queen when she stays in her castle there, or Cernunnos, master of the beasts and wild creatures, known as Cernenus in Dorset. He may be a Celtic Hercules waiting with his club in the sun. Helith may derive his name from the word 'Hel' making him a sort of underworld god, or it may come from the Saxon *helan* which means hidden or secret, or it may be he is a marker for a road, in Welsh, *heol*. There are quite a few standing stones associated with the sun which have 'hel' or 'hele' or 'hal' in their names, so there may be a link with the sun, certainly it is the sun which fertilises the earth in spring and causes the growth of fresh leaves and plants.

Another giant is to be found on the Downs in Sussex, at Wilmington, where the Long Man, the largest representation of a human figure in the world is to be seen. He stands over 230 feet tall, and instead of the Cerne Abbas figure's great club, he holds a slender rod in each hand. Maybe he is holding open the door of

The Long Man of Wilmington, Sussex, stands framed between his surveying poles. (*Edwin Smith*)

the year, and like the Dorset figure his feet are pointing sideways, to his right, like the figures of the Egyptian Gods. Looking towards him from the gate that leads into the field at his feet you may notice a small, ridged hill, below and to your right of the giant. Although this doesn't seem very significant in itself, a number of the other chalk hill figures have a similar hill, which gets a mention in their own legends.

The Long Man doesn't appear to have any festivals associated with him these days, even the church fête doesn't give him a mention. Again there is a priory within his shadow, which is now a museum of farming equipment and items of local historical interest. A view from one of the upstairs windows neatly frames the Long Man among the trees. Like the Cerne Abbas Giant, this figure is cleaned up from time to time, to make sure his white outline is clear. Some of the figures have been covered with white concrete or pale bricks to make this easier. When they were scoured every seven years or so, there used to be a bit of a 'knees up', but again this seems to have been forgotten by now.

Not all the figures were men. T. C. Lethbridge, an archaeologist, who took a great interest in these hill figures, excavated the shape of Magog, the Mother Goddess, near Cambridge. Her huge, smiling face with big round eyes looks like a child's drawing of his mother. Magog sits side saddle on her horse and when excavated, was surrounded by a number of other figures. Sadly all Lethbridge's work is being undone by neglect and bad weather and now it is not possible to see the goddess figure in the earthworks at Wandlebury. In 1954 when Lethbridge began his search for this lost figure he had only legends to go on, for on the steep hillside there was nothing to show the position of the hidden chalk-cut figures. Instead of stripping turf and digging, the archaeologist probed with a long, thin metal pole to discover the outline of the shapes, smoothed by years of exposure, under the covering grass. Once the shape was determined and mapped from marker sticks, the actual dig began in 1955 but caused a lot of antipathy from other archaeologists who tried to attribute the face and figures to glacial action.

Magog, the Mother Goddess, is also a Moon Goddess for a crescent shape was found above her head. The Mother was adored and worshipped long before the Father of later, more monotheistic faiths, for everyone has a mother. Lethbridge thought the symbolic figures might be of the Moon/Mother Goddess and a Sun God and their juxtaposition might indicate they were associated with eclipses. Gog was yet another vanished Solar figure, this time on the Hoe at Plymouth, whence Drake set forth, after his game of bowls, to do for the Spaniards (who turn up in the song of the Hal-an-Tow play at Helston). Drake is another candidate for the leader of the Wild Hunt with its Yell or Hell Hounds, belling across the Devon skies. If you unpick one thread from any of these legends or ancient sites it will lead you surely, if in a roundabout way, to another place, another old god, or another significant symbolic figure. Gog is associated with the New Year, for Hogmanay in Scotland is his festival. Angus Og is the Sun God in Gaelic folklore, but these days he has been diminished and his name is only remembered in a less pleasant aspect, Og – ogre, a sort of giant demon.

Other great hill figures which are in some way tied in with old customs may well have been far more common than they are now. A year's neglect can wipe them out except in folk's memories. Figures have been cut out of red sandstone hillsides and shown up dark crimson on the green grass although most seem to have been white chalk. One of the weirdest figures still visible is in Berkshire, near Uffington. Instead of a tall warrior there is the great, galloping shape of a white horse, about 360 feet long, across the top of a steep valley. Many of the figures are simple linear shapes, outlining in white against green the man or animal they depict. This famous horse is fragmentary, curved lines, deeply etched into the underlying chalk, forming the ears, part of the face, curving neck and arched tail, and separate legs, stretched out across the hillside. Like the representational art forms on Celtic coins, this disjointed creature looks perfectly clear, an obvious animal shape, but best seen from high in the air. One wonders how the original artist decided he had got his lines and markings exactly right.

Guy Underwood, who used the technique of dowsing not only to locate water in the usual way of water divining, but with a willow twig or other instrument, managed to detect traces of track lines and what he called 'aquastats'. Dowsing over the shape of this white horse Underwood traced a more horse-like, or even pregnant mare-like shape. Some students of the mysteries of hill giants have considered this particular beast is actually a dragon, which takes us back to the various legends of saints overcoming dragons or demons. Here at Uffington there is another link in the interwoven pattern, for there is a small mound below the horse shape, like that at Wilmington, apparently

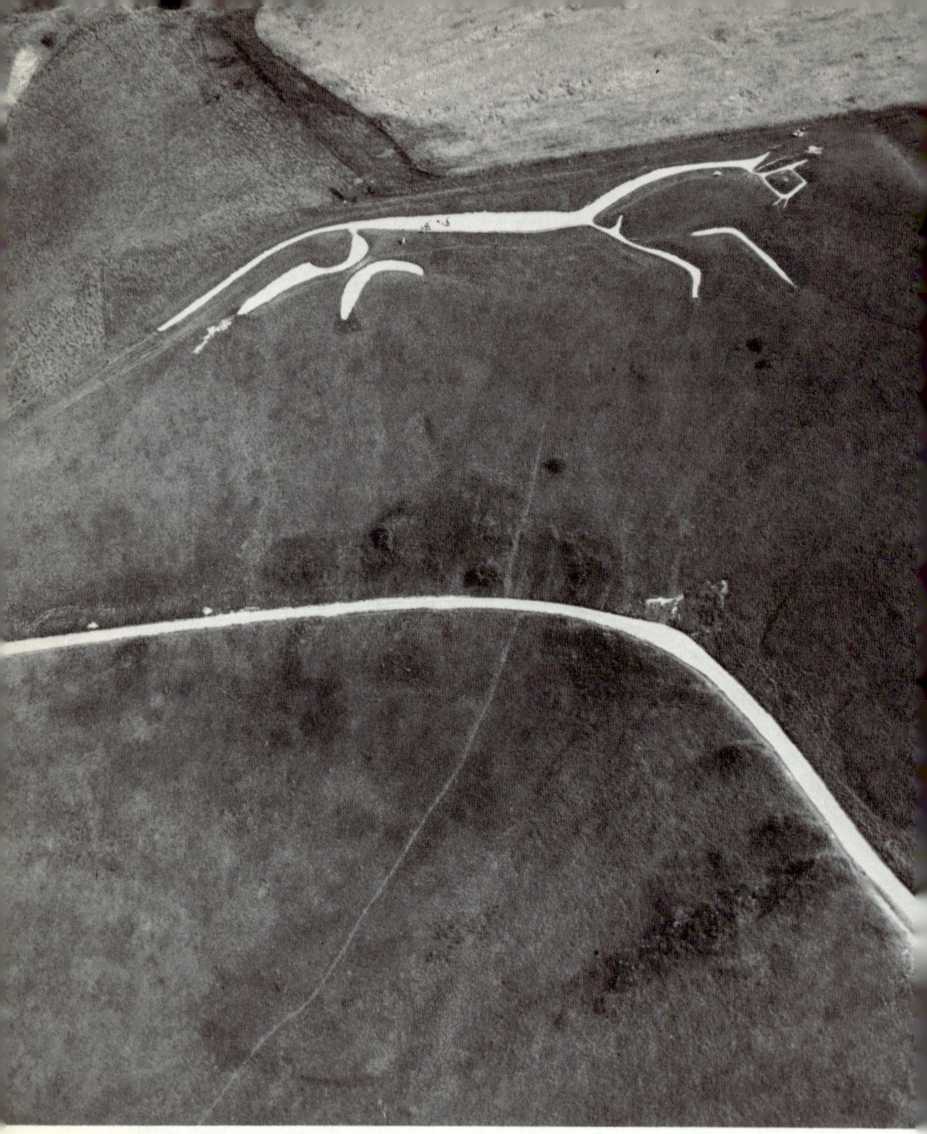

The White Horse at Uffington with its strange fragmentary Celtic art form is best seen from the air. (*Aerofilms*)

man-made, called Dragon Hill. A local legend tells how it was on this very spot that St George slew the Dragon, and where its blood ran in its death throes no grass will grow. The top of the small mound is still bare of grass. Maybe folk thought the horse was the saint's mount, or even a rough outline of the dragon, for the general shape could be a serpent with four legs and a pointed head. On the top of the gully on which the figure is carved is another 'Iron Age' hill-fort, rather like those above the heads of the Cerne Abbas Giant and the Long Man of Wilmington. Wherever these great chalk figures are found they seem to have these extra earthworks close by. Was the flat topped mound below, like a miniature Silbury Hill, a special viewing place or a site for some sort of ritual performance concerned with the hill figure? We just don't know. Perhaps the compound above these ancient chalk pictures contained the house of a priest or watcher who presided over the giant, keeping it clean and white, against the green grass.

Even the most modern of the big horses, that at Westbury in the Vale of the White Horse in Wiltshire, which was cut in 1778, is on a site which legend tells had an older, weirder, beaked horse/dragon shape. Here, too, there is an earthwork, Bratton Castle, somewhat bigger than those at Cerne Abbas and Wilmington. These are generally presumed to be Iron Age forts, constructed as defensive hilltop retreats, but they may well be

The prancing roundabout horse, seen at many fun fairs, is a reminder of the great totem White Horse, carved on Wiltshire hillsides.

older and have something to do with the great white figures they surmount. The sacred images of horses relate to the Goddess known to the Roman as Epona, but the white mare is yet another of the symbols of the Earth/Moon Mother, who was one of the earliest deities worshipped. Once again the thread vanishes into the general pattern of horse/dragon gods/goddesses which seem to crop up in some manner in a great number of the festivals which are still celebrated.

It is a great pity that we do not know if these vast figures were just boundary markers, or symbols of meeting places of various ancient tribes, or temples, open to the skies of the Great Father or the Earth Mother. Helith had his maypole dancers but that, too, has been given up. Each of these remote sites has its embanked space, at the top of the extremely steep slope, where a gathering could take place, for worship or just fun and games, a barbecue and country dancing, perhaps. Despite modern methods of agriculture and livestock husbandry, luck is still needed and it is well worth remembering that some of the ancient methods and arts are being revived, because they still work.

The nine men's morris to which Shakespeare was referring was a pattern cut out of the turf, which in Wiltshire was called a Mizmaze. The board of the game played with pegs called Nine Men's Morris has a similar maze pattern. In the old days there were dances when lines of individuals or couples formed a chain like the Conga and danced round the twisting path, marked by low banks. These ancient designs crop up all over the world, on rock carvings (there is one in Cornwall which I have not yet located) and on Cretan coins. Even the floor of Chartres Cathedral in France has this intertwined pattern in mosaic on the floor of the nave. In England there seem to be traces of the great maze path around Glastonbury Tor. The path there was not just a simple spiral although it might now appear to have been one, but a complex curved walk-way which bent back on itself at every turn, making seven levels of paths up the steep hillside. None of the actual trackway was very steep, though.

If you imagine the sort of shape of the leaves tight curled within a bud you will get an idea of the form. As the pilgrim walked or danced along the path, perhaps meditating as do monks in their square cloister walks, he would find the path suddenly double back on itself and wind back round the hill in the opposite direction. Eventually he would find himself at the top of the hill, in the centre of the maze. A column of participants would not get

Part of the circle of standing stones at Avebury, Wiltshire, within the ditch and embankment of the ceremonial enclosure. (*British Tourist Authority*)

entangled for they would be passing each other, some going deosil (clockwise), others widdershins (anticlockwise) round and back again, always gaining height. Archaeological evidence indicates there may well have been a circle of standing stones on the top of the Tor long before the first chapel dedicated to St Michael was raised there. At Avebury, that vast earthen bank which encircles a deep ditch, still about 20 feet from rim of the bank to the bottom of the dry ditch, even after nearly 5,000 years of weathering, there is another serpentine way. Old prints of this enormous ancient site, which encloses a whole village, show two winding ceremonial ways, once lined with standing stones.

There are dozens of stone circles, or more properly, the more complex geometrical shape of an ellipse, scattered throughout the British Isles. Only gradually are these rings, erected in antiquity, being understood for there are no inscriptions explaining their use so far discovered. Some are now considered to be concerned in marking time, for as the sun or moon rises over or between certain stones exactly, it would indicate a precise moment of the solar/lunar year. 'At the third stone, it will be midsummer, precisely!' If time mattered then there were probably some sorts of rites or festivals to celebrate at particular times of the year. Many of the circles of standing stones have cheerful names, like the Merry Maidens, the Giants' Dance, the Blind Fiddler, the Whispering Knights, the Rollright Stones. Many of these collections of upright boulders have tales about moving about in the night, or at midsummer or during eclipses. Some are supposed to roll down to a nearby stream or pool to drink, others were originally people turned to stone for breaking the Sabbath. There are tales about how difficult it is to exactly count the number of markers and so on, giving the rocks a semblance of life of their own. In Gloucestershire there is one monolith called the Tingle Stone which seems to have an 'electric' current running through it, and at certain times will seem to give a shock similar to that obtained when you brush your hand against a doorknob or other metal object after walking on nylon carpets – a discharge of static electricity. Tests with magnetometers on some of the old boulders have shown that they do have fields of energy about them. Certainly a sensitive dowser, using either a pendulum, at its simplest just a small weight on a piece of thin string, can get distinct reactions from different levels of such stones. Tom Graves has done some research into this and discovered that some tall rocks have as many as seven bands of differing charge from the surface of the ground to the top. He has even experimented to discover that these change their polarity as the moon changes phase, or alter after a certain period of time, perhaps taking a few minutes to reverse. He details some of his work in *Needles of Stone*.

Many of the stones used in ancient rings seem to be either crystalline or contain quartz. Now quartz crystals, because of the regular pulse they give off when subjected to a small electric current, are used to regulate many modern watches as well as scientific timepieces which keep accurate time over long periods. Did our ancestors have some notion of this fact, and discover that if a circle or ellipse of the right kind of rocks was constructed it would be possible for a priest or sensitive member of the tribe to be able to feel pulses or 'shocks' at specific moments? One dowser was so strongly affected by the force coming off a stone he was actually flung sideways from it. A film of this was shown on television. Dowsing is quite an easy skill to master and can provide many hours of interesting research, looking for underground water, or treasure. T. C. Lethbridge used a pendulum with different lengths of string to dowse over archaeological sites and discovered the positions of items of different metals or stone before they were uncovered by spade work. Guy Underwood traced the outlines of several hill figures with a springy rod, as well as finding blind springs, that is water runnels which do not surface, under many sacred or holy places. These seem to be shown by incurling spirals, which takes us back to the Helston Furry spiral, and the symbols carved on ancient kerbstones at Newgrange in Ireland. In Scotland there are series of circles chipped into boulders with a deep impression in the centre of the circles and straight lines crossing them. We don't know what these mean although it could symbolise the force fields around special stones, or stars in the sky or springs of fresh water.

At Avebury the great standing stones, some about 15 feet high, are of basically two shapes. There are strange diamonds, stood delicately on one corner alternating with narrower, more pillar-like stones. Male and female, perhaps, or positive and

A dragon, carved on a church pew end, recalls the legends of great flying, fire breathing serpents found all over the world.

negative? What would happen if a long line of dancers wound in and out of these tall markers, or whirled round in magical dance as do the modern witches, to raise power for their spells? Would it be possible to charge up these great boulders like some sort of accumulator battery, and store 'earth force' somehow? Tom Graves is sure that barrows and tumuli which are usually considered to have been primarily burial mounds, were in some way concerned with the weather. When the nineteenth-century 'barrow diggers' went out and opened up two or three mounds in the course of a day, they often encountered pretty wild thunderstorms, right overhead, to dampen their spirits. There is so much we just don't know about what our forbears were up to. We now have only legends of dragons and knights or angels who slew them. We have tales of stones dancing or moving at particular times of day or night or during the year. We have the evidence of a skilled race of mathematically minded people who could design a timepiece which still indicates the seasons

The pagan spirit of Nature with leaves issuing from his mouth is often seen as a roof boss in old churches, showing the blending of the two faiths.

accurately after 4,000–5,000 years. We still have survivals of some of their ancient feasts, especially in the beginning of May, when life returns to the earth. If you trace the Great Dragon Line from St Michael's Mount off Cornwall across the land and are able to get yourself to a place where you can see at least two or three of the landmarks on the line, in early May you would find the sun rising along that line.

There are revivals of some old customs and traditional events being brought back into use. If you happen to be about during the summer you might well discover you are in the right place to watch armoured and mounted knights jousting, and recapture something of the atmosphere of a medieval tourney. The British Jousting Society puts on a number of shows each year and it is fascinating to watch as the knights thunder together, lances couched, mail and surcoats glittering in the sun, and hear the clash of spear on shield and the crunch as one of the combatants is cast to the ground. It is not the same as the real thing though, for the lances are blunt, the contestants professional stunt men, for the most part, and their armour fibreglass or modern tough resin. They put on a brave show but it lacks the electric atmosphere of a real mêlée or tournament when sudden, bloody death occurs before your eyes. This is a spectacle, an entertainment and you are in no way involved. There is nothing like the feeling to be found at the simplest country school May Queen crowning or any of the older, traditional celebrations. The modern knights may be exciting to watch, but then so is any sport which involves speed or daring. Witnessing a festival is very different. There your heart and soul seem to get involved, your feet are impelled to move to the rhythm of the music, you are enchanted and involved and all other thoughts are completely banished from your mind.

It is not possible to explain what being at one of these old festivals will do to you. No doubt some folk attend these annual gatherings and come away unmoved and disenchanted, but most of the people who do make an effort to get up before dawn to be in at the start of the celebration, or who stay up all night, watching and waiting for the rituals to be performed gain something. Some people may be upset by the idea that pagan rites can continue in this Christian country, but the spirit of Nature is not sectarian, the reawakening of the land in spring is for everyone, a new miracle each year from the hand of the Creator. Many of the old celebrations were quelled forever during the Reformation, but many survived this bleak period of religious strictures, and when folk were allowed, again they set up their maypoles, and danced on the village greens. Today many customs have faded to become the church fête, but some of the traditional trimmings have turned up, even in this guise. Usually there is dancing, perhaps the local Morris Side puts on a show, and fancy dress for the children, the roasting of a ram or ox, maybe a simple play enacted under a summer sky (in Church Hall, if wet!) These are all parts of the old festivals, and should be preserved and reinforced. You can buy your luck from the Morris Men for a pittance (less than a packet of cigarettes, and they certainly offer neither life nor luck!) You can absorb something of the atmosphere of these feasts if you are able to get to them, for they are celebrations of the life-force, the marriage of the sun and the earth, call it what you will. These celebrations help to reunite man with his home planet, to encourage in him a feeling for the natural tides of the year, keep his feet on the ground and fill him with wonder. That has been one of our greatest losses, that sense of child-like awe at the workings of the seasons. Our ancestors must have had it, for they began many of the festivals which are still celebrated. We have the chance to preserve it and strengthen it, before the things we are doing to the Earth make it unpleasant to live on.

Some of these festivals are concerned with collecting for charities, or request money to restore the church roof. Don't be put off by that, for if you are there you are buying a share of the life-force. That is the warmth of the sun, the spirit of nature which dresses the bare winter trees in the gowns of new greenness, fills the summer sky with exalting larks, whose Midas finger turns the autumn leaves to gold. It is that spirit which can lift up our hearts, bowed down under snow-filled winter noons, at the sight of a first crocus, purple or golden among the black twigs of February.

If you are lucky enough to live in a place which does have its own festival or where there is talk of a revival or new celebration, do get involved. These recurring gatherings are important to the very spirit of the land. There can never be too many festivals, for something must be happening all the year round which is either a joy of itself, or a wonder to look forward to. May your own harvest of festivals be a fruitful one.

Bibliography

Ashe, G. (1971) *The Quest for Arthur's Britain*. Paladin.

Bord, J. and Bord C. (1972) *Mysterious Britain*. Carnstone Press.

Caine, Mary (1978) *The Glastonbury Zodiac*. Grael Communications, Torquay.

Cliffe Bonfire Society Programme (1978).

Cunnack, E. M. (1972) *Helston Furry Dance*. Flora Day Association.

Edwards, G. (1970) *Hogmanay and Tiffany*. G. Bles.

Frazer, J. G. (1922) *The Golden Bough*. Macmillan.

Graves, T. (1977) *Needles of Stone*. Turnstone.

Hawkins, G. (1965) *Stonehenge Decoded*. Souvenir Press.

Hole, C. (1970) *British Calendar Customs*. Batsford.

Lethbridge, T. C. (1975) *Gogmagog, The Buried Gods*. RKP.

Maltwood, K. (1974) *Glastonbury's Temple of the Stars*. J. Clarke.

Palmer, G. and Lloyd, N. (1972) *A Year of Festivals*. Warne.

Rawe, D. R. (1976) *Padstow's 'Obby 'Oss*. Lodenek Press.

Roberts, G. (1976) *Glastonbury*. Rider.

Ross, A. (1974) *Pagan Celtic Britain*. Cardinal.

Screeton, P. (1975) *Quicksilver Heritage*. Paladin.

Underwood, G. (1968) *The Patterns of the Past*. Museum Press.

Valiente, D. (1973) *ABC of Witchcraft*. Robert Hale.

Watkins, A. (1926) *The Old Straight Track*. Methuen.

Index